In a world where sexuality has become
this book is greatly needed. I wish every
read *Hedges* with an open heart and establish his own hedges to
protect himself from the tragedy of idol worship.

GARY CHAPMAN, PhD, author of *The 5 Love Languages*

In this new edition of *Hedges*, Jerry Jenkins has given us a strong
defense of marriage, needed now more than ever. In this timely
book, Jerry offers practical advice rooted in timeless biblical
principles on how to cultivate a strong, healthy marriage and
protect it from the thorns that threaten to choke and destroy it.
If your highest aim and heart's desire is to honor Christ and to
love and cherish your spouse till death do you part, then *Hedges*
is just the book for you—and it might ultimately save your
marriage and family and spare you a lifetime of heartache and
regret. Read it, reflect upon it, and, as Jerry wisely recommends,
start planting some hedges.

MIKE PENCE, forty-eighth vice president of the United States

In a world where literally anything goes, where marital status
seems inconsequential when compared to sexual desires and
feelings, where pornography is deemed a necessary stimulus for
boredom in marriage, where the workplace or classroom offers
illicit opportunities for exciting flirtation, how can Christians
commit to holiness and purity? In *Hedges*, Jerry Jenkins gives
incredible, practical wisdom for guarding the reader's most
treasured relationships. While this book is written for men, it will
be eye-opening and beneficial for women as well. It was for me.

ANNE GRAHAM LOTZ, bestselling author and international speaker

I kept nodding and saying "Yes!" as I read *Hedges*. My wife,
Nanci, is now with Jesus, and not a day goes by when I am not
profoundly grateful that we kept our vows to each other. True,

God will forgive those who ask Him, but don't set yourself up for a lifetime of regrets. Stay away from the cliff, because if you fall over, you may spend the rest of your life trying to take what you broke—and *who* you broke—and get it fixed. The good news is not only the resources we have in Christ and His family but in taking action, in step with the Holy Spirit, to protect our vulnerable minds and hearts from sexual temptation. My friend Jerry Jenkins has done an immense service to us in this book.

RANDY ALCORN, bestselling author

Jerry often gives advice about writing gripping fiction: "Get your character in terrible trouble." *Hedges* is a nonfiction book aimed at a man's heart to keep him from experiencing that terrible trouble in his marriage and family life. If you want a rich, lasting relationship, take his advice.

CHRIS FABRY, author of *Saving Grayson* and host of *Chris Fabry Live* on Moody Radio

Most of us read for information or pleasure, but how often do we have the opportunity to read a book with the power to change our lives? *Hedges*, the latest offering from Jerry Jenkins, is that book for the man who has the desire to dramatically increase his understanding and implementation of principles that will turn an average marriage into a great one. Read this one with a highlighter.

ANDY ANDREWS, *New York Times* bestselling author and founder of Wisdom Harbour

Jerry Jenkins is your friend. I know this because he has written this book. He admits he wrote it as a strong reminder to himself of the importance of protecting his own marriage. Then he boldly steps out to speak this truth to you. He dares to reveal the unvarnished reality of temptation, for many years successfully protecting himself from thinking like a fool and acting stupid. As a man, he gets it. And speaks it.

Only a true friend would risk having this conversation with you and me. And even though "hedges" sound like shrubbery, they're more robust. A lot more. This landscaping is priceless. These bushes could save your marriage. And your life. Crawl over them or snip your way through them at your own peril. Honor them and it will mean pure joy. I promise.

ROBERT WOLGEMUTH, author

Enemies of our marriages are all around us, and just being a Christian isn't enough to protect us. Jerry Jenkins provides honest and practical insights into the threats that would destroy our homes. Then he provides seven powerful hedges to enable us to fend off these assaults. No matter how strong your marriage, every man needs to read this book.

AL JANSSEN, author of *Your Marriage Masterpiece*

Jerry's distinction between "falling in love" and what love actually is alone is worth the price of this book. *Hedges* is a priceless gift Jerry has given to the body of Christ. He says this book is just for men. As one who has done premarital and marriage counseling for forty years, I disagree. It's a tremendous asset to high school students, college students, singles out of college, and premarrieds, as well as married couples. These hedges provide a way to bless and protect your marriage while simultaneously glorifying God in your marriage.

DR. CLARENCE SHULER, president and CEO of BLR: Building Lasting Relationships

Right before I married my beautiful wife, Lisa, someone gave me the book *Hedges* by Jerry Jenkins. That was more than thirty years ago. It helped me tremendously! I have given that book to many young people. Now to have it updated for a new generation is not only good but so needed for this current culture.

ERNIE HAASE, singer and recording artist

In *Hedges*, Jerry Jenkins sounds like a beloved head coach encouraging his players to stay alert and do your best! If you care about protecting and improving your marriage, this book is for you!

BO MITCHELL, NBA and MLB team chaplain

My wife and I, like Jerry and Dianna, have been married more than fifty years. To what do we attribute this milestone? First and foremost to our personal relationships with the Lord, along with the guidance and conviction of His Holy Spirit, His holy Word, and His people. Second, Jerry's book *Hedges*. My copy from 1989 is dog-eared because I read it front to back every few years and refer to it often. Men, if you want your marriage not only to survive but to thrive, don't miss learning and applying the principles and lessons found in this newly updated treasure chest.

WALT LARIMORE, MD, family physician and bestselling author of *The Best Medicine* and *The Best Gift*

HEDGES

7 WAYS TO LOVE YOUR WIFE & PROTECT YOUR MARRIAGE

JERRY B. JENKINS

A Focus on the Family resource
published by Tyndale House Publishers

To Dianna, of course

Contents

Acknowledgments

Thanks to John Perrodin for research assistance and for writing the study guide.

Thanks to Larry Weeden at Focus on the Family for believing in the project, championing it, and editing it.

Thanks also to Brandy Bruce for copyediting.

Thanks to my agent, Alex Field of The Bindery Agency.

Thanks to my son Dallas and daughter-in-law Amanda for writing the foreword.

Foreword

As his eldest son and daughter-in-law, we've known Jerry the father, Jerry the grandpa, and Jerry the author and speaker. But the most important role we've watched him play is Jerry the husband.

For decades we've had front row seats to Dad's devotion to his bride. He's honored Dianna, made her laugh, praised her to others, and remained passionately faithful. We pray our own children continue the legacy of commitment to godly marriage that Jerry inherited from his father.

And that's what this book teaches and celebrates: how to have *and keep* a godly marriage. As you read it, you'll find yourself increasingly eager to be a better spouse. Lucky for you, a major prescription for how to be one exists in these pages.

The guidelines in this book *will* make your marriage stronger. We've watched Dad and Mom and have seen what it looks like when a husband and wife truly live what they preach. We follow the same guidelines in our own marriage. We've heard countless others express how much this book has impacted *their* marriages.

This. Works.

But only if you're serious, because everyone begins their marriage wanting to be faithful to their spouse. Everyone wants to love and be loved, to feel safe and secure inside a passionate marriage.

But living it out for a lifetime is a different ball game. Considering how many relationships go awry, even inside the family of God, it's clear we need to avoid some land mines.

And if we're really smart, we'll avoid the areas in which land mines even exist.

In Matthew 5:29, Jesus says that if your right eye causes you to sin, tear it out. That shows how seriously God takes sin. Well, this book exists as a safeguard so you'll never have to contemplate such drastic action.

We have a vibrant marriage in large part because of the examples set by our parents and the lessons you're about to read. Lean in and absorb this wisdom, and start living it out today.

We're so glad we have.

Dallas & Amanda Jenkins
Creators, The Chosen

Introduction

A Necessity Bestowed

Let's get this on the table from the get-go: *Hedges* is a book for men.

Why? What is it men need? If you're at all like me, when you fell in love with the woman who is now your wife, you couldn't imagine getting your head turned again by any other woman. You were head over heels or over the moon or any other cliché that came to mind. It wouldn't have surprised you if you no longer even considered looking at another woman—friend, acquaintance, or stranger—regardless of how gorgeous or even sexy she appeared.

Until it happened. Oh, you were now married and still deeply in love, wholly committed to your wife and your vows. But that confounding wiring men seem to have in their brains made you look—once, maybe twice. You convinced yourself you were just appreciating beauty, and you fought impure thoughts.

But they crouched by your doorstep, didn't they? Why couldn't you have developed a set of blinders when you married? Your wife is worth the promises you vowed to keep. You don't even want to be tempted to stray. I hear you. I've been there. I don't want to blame it on gender, but it sure seems that men—devout believers or not—are programmed for frustration in this area. If that's you, too, stay with me.

That's not to say women haven't read *Hedges* and told me they've benefited from one of its previous iterations, the first having been released more than thirty-five years ago. But I'm a layman, not a Bible scholar, psychologist, or counselor. And neither do I pretend to speak for women, though I have learned much from my precious wife in more than a half century of marriage.

Frankly, that I am merely a writer—a novelist and biographer—has proved an advantage in this endeavor. I come at this as a fellow struggler, not as an expert. I want to be Bible based, of course, but not heavily theological, and certainly not theoretical. I'll leave the psychology to those so trained and will try to emphasize the practical. Bottom line, I want to provide handles, something to grab on to, something you can use to protect your marriage from infidelity.

Writing such a book back in the day resulted in my being asked occasionally to speak on the subject. Like a doofus, I started by trying to break the ice by joking about the frivolous, surfacy differences between men and women. I even asked, by show of hands, whether husband or wife preferred the toilet paper to roll over or under the dispenser. Then, during breaks, husbands would privately pull me aside and pose questions like "Should I tell my wife about my affair, or would it be better not to hurt her?"

That quickly sobered me and changed how I approached speaking on the topic.

Despite enthusiastic response to earlier versions of *Hedges*, sad to say, offering men counsel on how to protect themselves against infidelity has never been as crucial as it is today. It could be you've lost count—as I have—of the number of friends and relatives and Christian leaders whose marriages have imploded. The household-name spiritual figures alone who have succumbed to sexual temptation could justify an entire book on that subject.

But neither is *Hedges* about that shameful epidemic. It's about laypeople, regular men like you and me.

Am I surprised that people have fallen? Hardly. Embarrassed

for the church? Of course. Saddened by what this means for the reputation of Christ? Yes. But mostly I'm frustrated that so many have missed the plain message of Scripture that the escape is easier than they thought.

What Exactly Do I Mean by *Hedges*?

While it's not as common today as it was when we baby boomers were growing up, planting hedges in a yard can be a valuable addition to any landscape. They're a row of closely spaced bushes, shrubs, or small trees that are pruned and trained to form a dense, linear boundary. This offers a wide array of benefits, including enhancing both the aesthetic and the functional aspects of your yard. Among other things, hedges provide privacy, define property lines, and mitigate the impact of strong winds.

By strategically planting a hedge, you can also shield your property from prying eyes. This natural barrier not only adds a layer of seclusion but also contributes to a more peaceful and tranquil environment. It might also keep you from coveting your neighbor's greener grass. (See the metaphor I'm going for here?)

Maintaining a healthy and thriving hedge requires effort, but the rewards are well worth it. Regular pruning is essential to encourage dense growth and maintain a neat appearance. Planting hedges in your yard is a multifaceted investment that can provide benefits for years, much like the personal hedges I recommend in this book.

Job 1:10 implies that Job was so richly blessed—before God allowed him to be tested—because God had built a hedge "around him, around his household, and around all that he [had] on every side."

Jesus told a parable about landowners who planted vineyards and protected them with hedges. When those hedges were crushed or removed, ruin came to the precious possessions of those landowners.

Because people are much more precious than land, we must keep from deceiving ourselves about our own resolve and inner strength. Instead, we should plant healthy marital hedges that keep love in and infidelity out.

Love Is as Love Does

As Dianna and I taught our three now-grown sons, being "in love" is a misnomer, a meaningless, heart-thumping rush that's fun while it lasts, yet it can feel so profound that no one will be able to talk you out of it. We wanted them to know in advance that crushes, infatuation, and puppy love are tricks of the mind and heart. But of course when it happens to you, it's different. "No one has ever loved anyone the way I love her," you'll say. "This is bigger, more cosmic, more real, spiritual, dramatic, deep."

Ever felt that way? In truth, maybe your feelings were based on more than just looks or even personality. You may have fallen in love with someone's mind, her way of expressing herself, or her body language.

It'll pass. It always does.

But when you're in the throes of it, you won't be dissuaded. "This is eternal," you'll say. "This is more real to me than my relationship with God."

I well remember the first time I fell in love. I was ripe for it. It was the summer before my junior year in high school. I'd had girl friends, someone to walk to class or talk to on the phone till my parents threatened to bill me. But I had not been "in love."

A family moved to town, and somehow I was enlisted to help them move in. Their daughter, who just had to be in college, was a leggy, fresh-faced, quick-smiling girl who loved to talk and listen and look you right in the eye, especially if she thought you, too, were in college. It emerged that we were the same age.

Fifteen. She would be a high school classmate.

The first time we shared a ride home from a church activity

and held hands for all of six or seven minutes, I was smitten. What a boon to self-confidence! A girl everyone could see was a knock-out was "going" with me! For days I could think of nothing and no one else. I doodled her name, found reasons to call her, wrote her notes, hung around with her.

I was in love. How could anything be more beautiful, more perfect?

It was fun while it lasted and remains a harmless memory. But here's the problem with my all-too-common story and the truth we men must face: Being "in love" is not love.

Love is not a feeling or even a state of being. Cold and unromantic as this may sound, I am not "in love" with my wife of more than a half century. Rather, I love her. Yes, I love her more than anyone else on earth. But it's not something I'm "in." It's an act of the will. It's something I do. It's also a vow I took and something I love to do. But it's a verb, and not a state-of-being verb.

Don't in any way misinterpret this to mean that I've saddled myself with a burdensome assignment. If you knew us for five minutes, you'd see that Dianna and I more than just seem to really like each other, talk to each other, touch each other, flirt with each other, and show affection to each other. In fact, we often still marvel at the fact that when the other enters a crowded room, we're thrilled. Even now, when we're with each other most of the day, we still start the day with an embrace and end the day with a kiss.

Ours is a love relationship, but the love is a verb, not a noun.

That first time I fell in love, what or whom was I in love with? I thought I loved the girl. But I hardly knew her! She looked great, and she smiled a lot. Looking back, I don't know whether I liked what she said as much as that she said it to me. I was in love with being in love. It felt great to be the object of someone else's attention, especially someone impressive to others. It did wonders for my ego. I confess that even today, I enjoy being married to a woman others also find wonderful and beautiful. But that's not the basis for love as a verb.

What I eventually discovered about my first "love" was that she had a more serious boyfriend back where she came from. He was older. In fact, he had a job, money, his own car. When my sensibilities were rocked by the realization that I was merely a diversion to her, a nice guy who flattered her, it was almost too much for my teenage mind to fathom.

How could the object of my pure and boundless love be less than perfect? I could have lived with an embarrassing laugh, a silly taste in music, some limited proclivity for academics. But there was someone else in her life—her true love (whom she eventually married)—and she thought that was okay!

I could have fought for her, competed, striven to show her I was the better long-term bet. But the more I got to know her, the more I realized we were poles apart in most values. Now what was I to do with my head-over-heels infatuation? Most men have been through this very dilemma in some form at some time or another. In my case, I eventually had to accept that I could not have been in love with her, because I didn't know her. And after I got to know her, I chose not to love her by my actions.

That wasn't the last time I fell in love. By the time I met Dianna, I had learned little about avoiding infatuation. I did know this, however: Those warm, fuzzy feelings that make feeling in love so monumental would pass. They always do.

I'm happy to say that what I felt for Dianna was lightyears ahead of what I had ever before felt for anyone. But even if it wasn't, that would have been okay too. I wasn't about to marry someone just because I was hopelessly in love, because that alone is not a good basis for marriage.

Though I dated Dianna for less time than anyone else I had ever dated, and though we were engaged within a few months and married inside a year, ours was the most open and honest and probing relationship I had ever had. This was a woman I knew I would want to love even after I had no choice. You see, when you're in love, you have little say in the matter. Your head and heart tell you that you, among all men, have finally found that perfect combination of looks and personality and character. You think of her all the time, your heart races when you talk to her, you want to melt when you touch her.

Yet you don't truly know her yet.

Now, I'm not in the least saying that once I got to know my wife, I lost all feelings of love for her. In truth, I feel abundantly blessed, because Dianna has proved so easy to love. But that blind, head-over-heels-puppy-love-crush-infatuation eventually faded as it always does, and love became an action verb instead of a state of being.

Before when I said, "I love you," I could have just as honestly said, "I'm crazy about you. I idolize you. I can't help myself. You're everything to me."

Now when I say, "I love you," I'm saying, "I choose to put you ahead of me. I want you to have what you need. I want to do a dirty job you'd rather not do. I want your life to be better because I'm here to make it so. Can I pick up the kids? Can I run an errand? Can I save you some time, some grief, some discomfort? What can I do to show, to prove, to flesh out my love for you?"

All right, I'm flirting with fiction here, because, as you might suppose, I'm simply not that wonderful. Too often I let Dianna act out her love for me and make my life easier. I sometimes have to remind myself to put her first, to consider her better than I. But I know the principle, and I'm working on it.

That's what makes affairs so tenuous and maddening. A man who knows he is to act out his love for his wife suddenly finds himself infatuated with someone else. The lunacy of puppy love, gushy love, obsessive love takes him back to his halcyon days, and he forgets that this kind of so-called love will pass.

Oh, but not this one, no sir! This is so magical that God has to be in it, even though it flies in the face of everything He has said about deception and adultery and divorce. If only we could look down the road a year or two at the chaos that results from this . . . marriage broken, children devastated, and the "in love" fantasy over.

I can't say it too many times. True love, pure love, unconditional love is not something you fall into. Love is an act of the will. Love is as love does. Don't be "in" love. *Love.*

I had to bring up unconditional love, didn't I?

No way around it: Unconditional love is divine. Literally. We finite human beings are simply incapable of pure, unconditional love. It's a God concept, and at the risk of seeming flippant, may I say it's one of His best.

God's love is perfect. It is not infatuation. He does not have a crush on us. The Bible doesn't say, "For God was so in love with the world that He gave . . ." Rather, Scripture says that God loved us (action verb) in spite of ourselves. He knew all about us and loved us just the same. "God demonstrates His own love toward us, in that while we were still sinners, Christ died for us" (Romans 5:8).

Some translations say that God "extended His love toward us," and others say that He "showed His love to us." None say that God was so enamored with us that He was blind to our faults and thought we were wonderful. His is real love, unconditional love, the love of a Creator whose creations have broken His heart. Yet He loves us to the point of death, the death of His Son on the cross.

I wish I could fathom, let alone model or even explain, that kind of love. God loves the unlovable, people no one could like. Another biblical example of that kind of love is the father in Jesus' parable of the Prodigal Son. That father could not have liked his son. His love for his son was clear, but who could like a boy so selfish that he wanted his share of the inheritance early? He wanted to leave and do his own thing. He was selfish, wasteful, insensitive.

A father today, caught in the same bind, would say, "If this money wasn't legally yours, I'd never let you have it. You've been a rotten kid all your life, and now you're going to leave the best situation you could have and squander your fortune."

Do you think it was a surprise to the father of the prodigal that his son returned? I don't. He knew that boy. He watched for him. It wasn't a matter of *whether*, it was a matter of *when*. He might have hoped his son would come back happy and prosperous, but he knew better. He couldn't have liked him or liked what he had done, but the father's love was unconditional.

One of the hardest things that man had to accept was that his son was turning his back on his father's counsel. He would have helped the boy, taught him, shown him, done anything to make him secure. Still, when the son returned from dragging his father's name and fortune through pig slop, how did the father react? "Oh, sure! You run off against my wishes, squander the fortune I provided for you, and now you come crawling back expecting me to bail you out!"

No, you know the story. There was a ring for his finger, a robe for his back, a fatted calf for his belly. There was even a jealous brother. Unconditional love is worth being jealous of.

What the jealous brother didn't realize, of course, was that he, too, was loved unconditionally. He simply had shown love for his father by not putting his father's love to such a severe test.

Nothing in life is sadder than unconditional love pushed to its limits. By definition, it has no limits, but that is where the supernatural work of God's Spirit comes in. Because we are human, finite, and frail, we don't have it in us to love unconditionally.

As in romantic love, this love is as this love does.

Only God can love someone unconditionally, and we should each long to be His instruments in loving our spouses and children in that way.

Loving Is Doing

So, if I'm right that love is an act of the will, that means it cannot be demanded or required or commanded. It can only be bestowed. And that's why I have a list of rather prudish rules that I used to be embarrassed to speak of except to Dianna, to whom they are a gift of love.

These rules are intended to protect my eyes, my heart, my hands, and therefore my marriage. I say that these rules appear prudish because my mentioning them when necessary has elicited squints, scowls, and not-so-hidden smiles of condescension. Clarifying them in print, I risk implying that without following my list, I would plunge into all manner of affairs.

I direct the rules initially toward appearances, because I've found that if I take care of how things *look*, I take care of how they *are*. In other words, if I am never alone with an unrelated female because it might not look appropriate, I have eliminated the possibility that anything inappropriate will take place.

In enforcing my own rules, I don't mean to insult the many virtuous women who might otherwise have legitimate reasons to meet or dine alone with me without the slightest temptation to have designs on me. One of the more disappointing developments from the famed #MeToo movement is that many women actually take offense at what has become known as the Billy Graham rule: not meeting with, traveling with, or dining with an unrelated female alone. Somehow this has become an offense and is considered demeaning to women, when in reality it is meant to honor them.

Simply hedges, that's all these rules are.

As much as people don't like to hear, read, or talk about it, the fact is that most Christian men do not have victory over lust. I have a theory about that. Scripture does not imply that we will ever have victory over lust the way we're expected to win over worry or greed or malice. Rather, Paul instructed Timothy, and thus us, not to conquer or stand and fight, or pray about or resolve against, but to *flee* lust (see 2 Timothy 2:22).

I know he specified youthful lust, but I don't believe he was limiting it to a certain age but rather describing it, regardless of the age lust occurs. The young man in me will have to flee lust until I flee life. And that's why I stated above that too many have missed the scriptural message that the escape is easier than they thought. Think about it. Isn't it freeing to know that even God advises us to simply flee? For how many years have we males resolved to quit lusting, to put away impure thoughts, to keep our minds pure regardless of what images the media might offer them? We've turned over new leaves in other areas of our lives. We may have become more sensitive, more helpful, more spiritual, better husbands, better fathers—yes, sometimes in large part because we decided to and applied ourselves.

But lust, this dirty little secret, bites when we least expect it and despite all our human efforts. What's wrong with us? Yes, God designed us this way, and yet there are clear biblical mandates against sexual impurity. Trying to conquer lust, and failing, is maddening, frustrating. Until we get the message from Paul that we aren't expected to even try.

Don't work at it.

Don't study it.

Don't pray about it.

We're given permission to flee!

Head for the hills. Run for your life.

I don't know about you, but that takes a lot of pressure off me. Oh, I'd much rather be known as a mature Christian who is above all that youthful lust. It gives me no pleasure to have to say, "Sorry, you've got the wrong guy." But at least I don't have to suffer and fail over and over because I just can't manage. I don't have to manage. All I have to do is flee.

That tells me that God understands. He gave me these triggers, these eyes, these hormones, this libido, and not solely for my own gratification. And He designed all this so well that He can't even trust me to be a faithful steward of it. He wants me to be, of course, and He instructs me to be. But in my own strength, I fail every time. And instead of condemnation, God offers an out. An escape. Literally. Flee. You've got to love that.

Now, to be realistic, I don't want to be turning tail and running all the time. That's a great out when temptation sneaks up on you, but to me there's wisdom in planning ahead, in planting hedges against situations that lend themselves to temptation.

My Hedges

I have planted hedges around myself to protect me, my wife, my family, my publishers, my church, and supremely, the reputation of Christ. I share them not to boast but to admit that I'm still fleeing and in the hope that they might be of some benefit to you. (I'll expand on them in part two.)

Here, then, are my personal hedges:

1. Whenever I need to meet or dine or travel with an unrelated woman, I make it a trio. Should an unavoidable last-minute complication make this impossible, my wife hears it from me first.
2. I am careful about touching. Although I might shake hands or squeeze an arm or shoulder in greeting, I embrace only dear friends or relatives, and only in front of others.
3. If I pay a woman a compliment, it is on clothes or hairstyle, not on the person herself. Commenting on a pretty outfit is much different, in my opinion, from telling a woman that she herself looks pretty.
4. I avoid flirtation or suggestive conversation, even in jest.
5. I remind my wife often, in writing and orally, that I remember my wedding vows, especially this one: "Keeping you only unto me for as long as we both shall live." Dianna is not the jealous type, nor has she ever demanded such assurances from me. She does, however, appreciate my rules and my observance of them.
6. When our sons were young, I maintained a rigid hedge around my time. From the time I got home from work

until the children went to bed, I did no writing or other work. That gave me lots of time daily with the family and for my wife and me to continue to court and date.

With the new century, this sixth hedge became moot. I am now a full-time freelance writer, and the boys are no longer living at home. So that last hedge has become this: I keep myself accountable to a small board of trusted friends. More about that later.

For now, let me suggest another, seventh hedge you may want or need to plant for this century, due to the insidious nature of internet porn. It's simply this: Do anything and everything to avoid pornography.

Unfortunately, as I've implied, that has become nearly impossible these days. You can stumble upon it unawares, or—if you're tempted to justify it for a momentary rush—not even the old shame of being seen in a porn shop or adult theater can stop you. Access to this poison is as easy and convenient as a keystroke on your computer.

But the wholly private nature of it won't eliminate the regret and shame that will haunt you if you're a true believer who desperately wants to honor God and your marriage. And I'll get to practical suggestions for what I mean by doing "anything and everything" to avoid it.

Let me clarify: My hedges may not be your hedges. Especially nowadays, you may need to plant some where I never dreamed they would be needed, and vice versa. Resist the urge to get caught up in what a weak, paranoid guy I must be. Rather, if my hedge applies, plant it; if it doesn't, plant one of your own where you need it.

Your marriage, and the Kingdom, will be the better for it.

Jerry B. Jenkins, 2024

PART ONE

WHY WE NEED
HEDGES

Sometimes the thing we most need

protection from is ourselves.

1

WHEN FIRST WE PRACTICE
TO DECEIVE

I once saw a subtle, most insidious television commercial, though it wasn't sexy, lewd, or vulgar. In fact, it dripped with respectability. A handsome, distinguished, middle-aged man is talking by phone from a commercial jet, telling his boss, we assume, that the next business trip he's been assigned falls on his wedding anniversary. "So you," he says in essence, "can tell my wife."

Cut to the business trip where he's in charge, salvaging the project, the local workers appearing grateful that he came.

Afterward, he's in an airport, on his phone again, telling his boss he's on his way home. "Osaka!" the man says.

Next we see him in Osaka.

Then we hear him telling the boss that it's his son's birthday. "Promise you won't call me."

Cut to preoccupied Dad gazing at a cake with unlit candles, party decorations all about. A look comes over him when the phone rings. And next we see him somewhere else—leading, controlling, succeeding. A champion.

In the space of sixty seconds, one of our leading airline companies—with the voice of an Academy Award–winning actor in the background—has sent us a message loud and clear. They're saying they will take care of us when our job is more important than our wife. When a crisis overseas is more important than getting home, they'll get us there in style. When the boss's call takes precedence over our child's birthday, we can count on them to make our trip enjoyable.

The point is clear: The top priorities for a man today are his job, his career, his status, his ability, his talent, and where those things will take him. This man in the commercial is someone important, someone crucial. He chooses the right airline because the people of that airline understand all this. And why shouldn't they? In a few years, they'll be flying his children between his home and his former wife's home.

Somehow, the tasteless commercials are easier to deal with than this one. We know it's a myth when we see a couple dozen sun-drenched hipster creatives cavort as if a lite beer makes their day. We've never seen that many good-looking people in one room at one time in our lives, let alone happy. And if we've ever seen that many people drinking at the same time, we have an idea how many of them will still be smiling by the end of the evening. More than likely, we'd find some in the bathroom, some on the floor, and too many behind steering wheels.

We can also deal with commercials that glorify sexuality in any context. They are so overt, so brazen, from a young man and woman dancing like superstars in the middle of a brewery to three voluptuous ladies singing and dancing with a black-eyed dog.

Those are easy to pass off or turn off. But what do we do with the man so indispensable that his family comes second? Don't we want to be like him? Wouldn't that be something? To be on call any time of the day or night to be flown somewhere in the world where only we can solve the critical problem? The wife will understand. The kids are resilient. And aren't we, in the long run, really doing it for them anyway? The photography, the color, the acting, the music, the script, the narrator, even the company behind it all lend credibility, an air of authority, of rightness. But is it right?

"He who trusts in his riches will fall, but the righteous will flourish like the green leaf. He who troubles his own house will inherit the wind" (Proverbs 11:28-29, NASB). I don't even know what it means to inherit the wind, but it doesn't sound good, does it? It sounds like death.

Enemies of Marriage

The enemies of marriage are all around and are increasing in number every day. In my young married days, porn marshalled itself in adult bookshops and seedy theaters. But this millennium boasts instantaneous internet porn, intimate chat rooms, and a constant barrage of immoral messages from movies and television.

Being seen parking near a porn shop would be hard to explain, let alone being seen trying to sneak into one, but that danger has been eliminated by the ubiquitous prevalence of online porn and so-called soft porn.

We'll see later that surveys of even pastoral staff alarm us with the percentage of clergy who admit to immoral addictions. The sexual revolution and moral relativism of the twentieth century have come home to roost in the twenty-first before our very eyes. Spiritual leaders fall. Friends, neighbors, and families split. Pain, suffering, and emotional devastation spiral out of control. Children of divorce not only suffer during childhood but often also continue the cycle into their own adult lives.

As I'm sure you know, being a Christian does not eliminate temptation from your life. Quite the contrary. As we'll also see

> The enemies of marriage are all around and are increasing in number every day.

later, statistics tell us that Christian marriages dissolve due to infidelity at a rate frighteningly close to those among people who claim no faith.

Not long ago a friend and his wife, pillars in the Christian community, went through a horrendous divorce. Not only were they and their children emotionally damaged, but the twenty-year-old ministry they had built together was also ruined. The wife, who had been praying for reconciliation, seems to have been hit the hardest emotionally. And it remains to be seen what lasting impact the divorce will have on the children. I truly believe that if this couple, particularly the husband, had been practicing some form of the personal hedges I'm trying to encourage in this book, their marriage never would have ended in divorce.

Sadly, few men believe they need to plant hedges until it's too late. Consider the following story, which I heard firsthand (the names have been changed).

Christopher and Ashley

Ashley was not the prettiest and certainly not the sexiest woman Christopher had ever seen. In fact, she didn't hold a candle to his wife. But Ashley worked for Christopher. He spent a lot of time with her at the office. He could tell she admired him. He liked her, respected her, and thought she was bright, creative, and interesting. He liked being around her, liked her smile, enjoyed her wit. She was doe-eyed, had perfect teeth, and was committed to her husband.

Was Christopher romantically interested in her? The very question would have offended him. They were both happily married. Neither would even think about an attraction between them. Christopher told his wife about Ashley from the day she was hired. His wife was eager to meet her and her husband, and the couples genuinely liked each other. The couples didn't socialize frequently because they lived too far from each other, but Ashley kept Christopher up-to-date on what was happening in her life, and Christopher told his wife. Christopher's wife talked on the phone with Ashley occasionally. Christopher wasn't starry-eyed about Ashley, and Christopher's wife had no reason to believe that Ashley held anything but respect for Christopher.

Which was true.

Was Ashley worth losing a home and family over? Now, there was a question even more insulting than the first. No woman was worth that. In fact, Christopher used to tease his wife, "If I ever throw you over, kid, at least I won't humiliate you by running off with a dog."

It was a joke because it truly was the last thing on his mind. He was a Christian, active in church, a father of three with a comfortable and happy life. He wasn't looking for anything more or anyone different. He was challenged, motivated, and excited about his job and his career path. He was solid. Christopher wasn't even going through a midlife crisis.

So he didn't worry when he first found himself missing Ashley when she was out of town for a couple of days. He asked his secretary to be sure to let him know when she called, because he had "business to discuss with her." It was true. And when the business had been discussed, they talked a little more.

"We miss you around here, Ashley." The emphasis was on "we."

"I miss you too," she said. "All of you. I look forward to seeing you when I get back."

"Me too."

Nice. Friendly. Innocent.

And dangerous. But Christopher didn't know that then.

When Ashley returned, her relationship with Christopher changed in subtle ways. During a meeting or in a room full of people, they could read each other in an instant. They weren't reading anything personal in each other's eyes. They just knew what the other was thinking about the topic at hand. Christopher could tell when Ashley was being circumspect. Ashley could tell when Christopher was just being polite, when he didn't really like a proposal but was kind in how he responded to it.

Christopher began to find reasons to be around Ashley. He also found reasons to touch her in a brotherly or even fatherly way— a squeeze of the hand, a touch on the shoulder, a hug of greeting or farewell. He would not have described this as sexual or even sensual. There was no more to it than any man's enjoying physical contact with an attractive, young female.

One day, Christopher was waiting for a cab to the airport as Ashley left the office for the day. "The airport's on my way home," she reminded him. "I'll give you a ride."

They talked business on the way. At the curb, he looked into her eyes and thanked her warmly. "Any time," she said. He held her gaze until the humor of her comment sank in. They both smiled. "You know what I mean," she said.

She meant she would do anything helpful for such a good friend. But both also began to like the intimate sounds of words that could be taken two ways. In the ensuing weeks and months, Christopher and Ashley slowly began to depend upon each other emotionally. He told her things no one else in the office knew: his assessments of others, his private ambitions, his plans, his dreams. They went from telling each other what good friends they were to making their conversation more personal, more meaningful. He called her his "favorite friend." She often told him he was "special."

Theirs wasn't a dual pity party, bad-mouthing their respective spouses or looking to the other for ingredients missing in their marriages. No, they were simply two people who hit it off, liked each other, became special to each other, and eventually became enamored with each other. Suddenly, or so it seemed, the inevitable happened.

They justified a few lunches and even a working dinner. When their bodies touched while in a cab or in a restaurant booth, neither pulled away. It was natural, familiar. Brotherly and sisterly.

When he touched her arm while talking to her, he often left his hand there even after his point had been made.

At a convention out of town, even with six others from their office along, they found opportunities to be alone together. It wasn't easy, and though their relationship had not escalated to the declaring stage yet, they both knew. There was no one either would rather be with.

After a late dinner one night with everyone from their office, Ashley called Christopher's room and said she couldn't sleep.

"I'm not tired either," he lied, though he had collapsed into bed after the long day. "What do you want to do?"

"I don't know. Just talk."

"So talk."

"You wanna go for a walk?"

They met in the lobby and strolled the deserted city streets. She thought her sweater would be enough, but the summer night grew chilly after midnight, and as they crossed a bridge over the river, he slipped his suit jacket over her shoulders. She smiled at him in the moonlight, and he put his arm around her. She slipped her hand around his waist. They walked silently for twenty minutes until they came to a dark spot between streetlights.

Christopher slowed to a stop, his emotions racing. Ashley looked quizzically at him, but when he took her in his arms, they embraced so naturally, so perfectly, that it seemed right. He could feel her heart pounding. "Dare I kiss you?" he whispered in her hair.

She held him tighter, as if stalling to decide. "Your call," she said, mimicking his favorite expression to subordinates. It was all he needed to hear.

Theirs was one long, soft, meaningful kiss that spoke volumes. They stared into each other's eyes for a slow moment, then headed back to the hotel, his hand gently on her arm. As the building came into sight. Ashley stopped. "We have to talk."

"I know," he said.

"What are you thinking, Christopher?"

"The same thing you're thinking."

"Don't be too sure."

"I'm sure, Ashley."

"You first, boss."

"This will never work, Ashley. It didn't happen. We should go back to our respective rooms, still just good friends who happen to like each other very much."

Her eyes filled. "You know me too well."

"I'm relieved, Ashley. I certainly didn't intend this, and I don't want to mislead you."

"The walk was my idea, but I didn't have this in mind."

"Nothing happened, Ashley. Deal?"

He stuck out his hand. She shook it but held on. "Why do I want to kiss you again, Christopher? I agree we have to end this, but it seems so incomplete."

"I feel the same way. But we cannot. We must not."

"I know," she said, dropping his hand. She smiled bravely and headed into the elevator.

Christopher stared at the ceiling until four in the morning, dredging up every negative detail of his marriage. In twelve years, he and his wife had become known as a successful and happy couple. By the time he gave up trying to sleep, however, he had convinced himself that he had never loved her, that the marriage was a mistake, and that he felt something for Ashley he had never felt for any other woman, including—and especially—his wife.

Jaw set and mind whirling, Christopher strode to the window and gazed into the darkness. Was that Ashley sitting on the low concrete wall in the courtyard below?

Christopher freshened up and dressed quickly. He took the stairs to the ground floor and exited through a side door. Ashley started when she first saw him. Then she sat still and stared ahead, as if resigned that this meeting was somehow inevitable.

"Ashley, are you all right?"

She nodded and dabbed at her face. "I just have to get over this."

"Anything I can do?"

She shook her head. "It's not going to be easy working with you."

"It doesn't have to be difficult, Ashley. We just need to back up a few months. We're friends, and we can enjoy that, can't we?"

"You make that sound easy, Christopher. I can't."

"Why not?"

She took a deep, quavering breath and fought for composure. She still hadn't looked at him. "I'm in love with you, Christopher. That's why."

He reached for her, and she came to him. They embraced and kissed, and he told her he loved her too. He led her back into the hotel the way he'd come, avoiding the lobby and the elevators. They trudged up the stairs to her room. He left there two hours later, in time to prepare for the day.

Christopher and Ashley shared a delicious, bleary-eyed secret for the rest of the convention. They spent most of every night together, and there was no more talk of how things would have to change when they traveled back home to reality.

Christopher and Ashley convinced themselves that their love was so perfect that even God would find favor in it—bless it.

Neither was prepared for the vehement reactions from their spouses and extended families. The anger, the confusion, the accusations drove them closer to each other. Within six months both divorces were final, and Christopher and Ashley were married. A year later, while Ashley was pregnant with her first child, Christopher announced he had made a terrible mistake. He wanted his wife and family back, and he set upon such an impractical and obnoxious approach that he lost both his new wife and his job. In the process, he permanently alienated himself from his former wife as well.

Surely Not Them!

Unfortunately, Christopher and Ashley's story is not unique. In fact, I've heard several similar to it from friends, relatives, and acquaintances. Not one of the individuals involved says they in any way set out to fall in love with someone else, have an affair, and break up their marriage. It just snuck up on them, they say. It just happened.

Such stories have become so common that I cringe when someone says, "Did you hear about so-and-so?" They may be informing me of a promotion or an award or a new baby, but my first dreaded thought is *Oh no, please, not them, too*. All too often, my worst fears are confirmed. No one is immune. The strongest marriage any of us know of is in danger today if hedges are not in place.

I recently reminisced with several old friends. Every one of us knew personally of several painful marriage failures due to infidelity. Even more appalling, nearly all of us could point to incidents among our close relatives. Can anyone still doubt there's an epidemic of divorce, even within the church and, sadly, rampant even among so-called Christian leaders?

Bizarrely, in the twenty-first century, the problem is exacerbated in the Christian community because unfaithful spouses are generally not in danger—the way the secular community is—of contracting sexually transmitted diseases. The type of person I'm writing about is not characteristically promiscuous. Christopher, in the above example, had never before slept with a woman other than his wife.

> The strongest marriage any of us know of is in danger today if hedges are not in place.

Try an informal survey on your own. Ask friends and relatives how many people they know who have fallen to sexual temptation. Perhaps you don't need to ask. Maybe, sadly, you know firsthand more such stories than you care to recount. If those people were vulnerable, who else might be? Who will be next about whom you say, "I never would have dreamed he would do such a thing"? You know these people. You have to wonder what made them fall. What made them vulnerable?

Little Foxes

Just as it's the little foxes that spoil the vine (see Song of Solomon 2:15), so seemingly small indiscretions add up to major traps. Christopher and Ashley allowed themselves to admire, like, respect, and enjoy each other without giving a second thought to the progression of their feelings, the danger of developing strong emotions, or the lure of infatuation. They never reminded themselves of their wedding vows, because they had no intention of breaking them. Desires and emotions sneaked up on them when they least expected it, and then it was too late.

Look at the account of David's failure in 2 Samuel 11. Here was a man after God's own heart. Have you ever wondered why he didn't go to battle? Scripture doesn't provide a lot of detail about this incident, but this question arises: Was David too old, too tired, too successful, or too something else to lead his army? Or was there some subconscious, or not so subconscious, maneuvering to get himself into a position where he could get next to Uriah's wife?

Why did he take a walk on his veranda that day? Was Bathsheba not aware that her bath was within sight of the king's palace? A stroll atop his palace and a bath in the open air could be considered nearly innocent indiscretions. Give Bathsheba the benefit of the doubt, but David should have turned away when he saw a naked woman. The fact that even a man after God's own heart was unable to do that lends credence to the theory that we are to flee rather than try to conquer lust.

Inviting the wife of your commanding officer over after seeing her bathe must be considered more than a small indiscretion. Despite my respect for a man of God, I have to suspect David's motives. Could he simply have wanted to get better acquainted? There's an understatement. He knew this woman. She was married to one of his high-ranking soldiers and lived in the neighborhood. Did David know when he invited her that he would sleep with her that night? Surely he wasn't testing his resolve to remain pure before God. What Bathsheba knew or didn't know we can scarcely guess. In that time, a summons from the king was disobeyed only under the threat of death. So, from the time she received his invitation, her fate was sealed.

Safe to say, had it not been for the initial indiscretions, adultery may never have resulted. And look at what happened after that. Bathsheba became pregnant. David called Uriah home from battle in the hope that he would sleep with his wife and believe the child was his own. Uriah, a man of honor (how must that have made David feel?), refused to enjoy the comforts of his home and his wife while his men were in battle. Had Uriah slept with his wife, David would have fostered deceit. As it turned out, Uriah's sense of duty drove David to have him killed. Scripture tells how David sent the Hittite back to war with his own death notice in his hand (see 2 Samuel 11:14-17).

The consequences are legendary. Talk about adultery creating chaos! David's wives went to another man. The son of the illicit union died. What did that mean for David's covenanted dynasty? Fortunately, he eventually responded with true repentance to the admonition of the Lord that came through the prophet Nathan.

So why did the child die? Because sin has consequences.

Perhaps to evidence God's forgiveness, Scripture soon refers to Bathsheba as David's wife, and their second son together was Solomon, whom "the LORD loved" (2 Samuel 12:24).

Close Encounters of the Worst Kind

How close have you come to being burned? Have you found yourself impressed with someone and then attracted to her? Maybe it seemed innocent and safe but then you said or did things you never would've thought you'd say or do. Maybe on a business trip you hung around with a colleague of the opposite sex and, upon reflection, know you wouldn't have wanted your spouse to do the same thing. It could be that nothing improper was said or done, but simply investing the emotional energy and time was inappropriate. Maybe, looking back, you see you were living dangerously. When friends fall right and left, you recognize you were lucky that you weren't ensnared.

Or maybe you did become emotionally or even physically involved and fell just short of committing adultery—or you did in fact go all the way. Perhaps you live with guilt because you never confided that to anyone, including—and especially—your spouse.

If so many of your friends and acquaintances have fallen—people you never would have suspected—how will you avoid becoming a casualty?

2

THE TWENTY-FIRST CENTURY

Into the third decade of this twenty-first century, there's a new openness to interaction between the sexes in the workplace, in the neighborhood, in counseling—even in the church. Christians touch each other more than I remember from my childhood. They speak more intimately too—they're closer to one another.

This has a healthy aspect to it. Sometimes I wonder what was wrong with us in the last century, appearing stoic to the point of frigidity. Surely it's healthier now to show genuine physical affection for brothers and sisters in Christ.

But there can also be grave dangers. Fear of too much or inappropriate intimacy can actually be a good thing.

The late Dr. Tim LaHaye and I were often asked if we thought it was fair to use fear in our Left Behind novels to, in essence, scare people into the Kingdom. When worded so starkly, of course that sounds bad. On the other hand, frankly, some things need to be feared. An eternity without God is one.

Dianna and I raised three sons, and I wasn't above scaring them about things they should be afraid of. I told them that if they played in the street, they risked being run over. If they played near the charcoal grill, they risked horrible burns. If they played with the electrical outlet, they risked electrocution.

Fear can be as good a motivator as any to maintain sexual fidelity to your wife. I have friends who say that the fear of being caught and exposed is enough to keep them from buying certain magazines and books, watching certain shows and movies, and even cruising questionable neighborhoods.

In a survey[1] conducted by Christianity Today International (CTI) researchers, of one thousand male readers (non-pastors) of *Christianity Today*, fully 23 percent indicated they had engaged in sexual intercourse with someone other than their wives. Twenty-eight percent indicated they had involved themselves in other forms of sexual contact outside their marriages.

In a separate survey[2] of pastors, 23 percent said they had done something sexually inappropriate outside their marriages, 12 percent indicating adulterous intercourse.

Ready for this? The above research was conducted more than twenty years ago! Internet porn was in its infancy then. In 2001, the CTI magazine *Leadership*'s "Survey on Pastors and Internet Pornography"[3] found that four in ten pastors online had visited a pornographic website, more than one-third of those within the previous twelve months. *Leadership* also reported this response to the statistics: from non-pastors, "So many!" and from pastors, "Is that all?"

They revisited this issue fifteen years later, only to find—according to an online study by the Barna Group, commissioned by Josh McDowell Ministry and Cru for an April 2016 summit—that of nearly 3,000 adults, teenagers, and pastors, most pastors (57 percent) and youth pastors (64 percent) admit they have struggled with porn.[4]

So what does the landscape look like today? Former pastor Ray Carrol, author of *Fallen Pastor: Finding Restoration in a Broken World*, conducted an anonymous survey following his own moral failure and found this issue even more pervasive now. He found that 33 percent of pastors admitted to infidelities of which their spouses still remain unaware. A separate study found that one in nine pastors admitted to having committed adultery.[5]

> Men who admit their weaknesses to one another gain strength and amass weapons against temptation.

Frankly, I hesitate to share such findings. On the one hand, they shed light on an epidemic. On the other, is there not a risk of providing justification? Might not a man be tempted to rationalize, *Even my pastor slips, so it's no big deal if I do too?*

Heaven forbid. To me, mutual accountability is key. In fact, as I mentioned, with my sons now grown and gone, this hedge replaces number six on my list: I will hold myself accountable to a board of trusted male friends charged with asking me any question they wish about my health, my spiritual life, my work life, and my marriage. They're free to ask:

Are you staying true to your wife?
Are you avoiding dangerous situations?
Are you able to flee temptation?

Knowing we're not alone in this struggle can make it easier to consent to accountability. Men who admit their weaknesses to one another gain strength and amass weapons against temptation. We are able to talk openly about what people like the couple in the first chapter could have done to insure against the misery they brought upon themselves.

Close friends and even relatives and loved ones report real victory through the hedge of accountability. (More on this in chapter 14.)

Fleeing Porn

As I implied earlier, probably the greatest change in society this century is the easy, private accessibility of pornography via the internet. Again, while we'd all like to believe we are above such a base temptation, the statistics above reveal otherwise. (Not to mention, we know ourselves.)

Fleeing this lure, if it happens to be one that troubles you, begins well in advance. This seventh hedge applies with or without an accountability board: Do anything and everything to avoid porn. Don't go to a website that can titillate you with sample images, rationalizing that at least you didn't pay to see anything worse. Anyone who has even happened upon these sites accidentally knows that the advertising alone far exceeds the bounds of propriety for a Christian.

It's amazing how many believers have been ensnared, caught, and even fired for accessing internet porn on the job. Imagine the humiliation and pain to their families, let alone to themselves.

There's nothing complicated about the hedge that needs to be planted here. Simply conduct an internet search for "Christian anti-porn websites," and check out all the options for apps that will help you slam the door on this poison. If porn is a temptation for you—as it is and has been for so many—you should find that the earlier such decisions are made for you, the more successful you'll be in fleeing.

Many such helpful resources actually monitor how you use your computer and will email a notice to your accountability partners should you log onto a porn site.

Focus on the Family offers internet filter recommendations at focusonthefamily.com/parenting/monitoring-internet-activity. With tools designed to monitor your family's internet use, you can plant hedges for yourself, too.

Let's Get Practical

If this is a hedge you need to plant—in essence, doing everything in your power to insulate yourself against streaming pornography—invest time in listing how you might go about this. Here are some suggestions (and these also apply to the shows and movies that stream into your home):

1. Install content filters. (See specific options below this list.)
2. Enlist an accountability partner. Can you be honest enough with your wife to seek her help in this?
3. Limit screen time. Avoid idle browsing.
4. Guard your thoughts. Prayerfully discipline your thought life. Ask God's indwelling Spirit to help you.
5. Make prayer and Scripture reading a daily habit.
6. Worship and fellowship. Spend time with fellow believers to foster community and mutual support.
7. Seek professional help if needed. Christian counseling from those with expertise on the subject can be greatly beneficial, especially if the counselor has personally wrestled with the temptation.
8. Reflect on the consequences. Consider the impact of pornography on your spiritual, emotional, and relational well-being.
9. Remind yourself of God's grace and forgiveness. Many struggle just as you do, and His grace is greater than your sin.
10. Be persistent. Galatians 6:9 admonishes us to "not grow weary while doing good, for in due season we shall reap if we do not lose heart." Stay committed.

Filter Options

While I have urged you to conduct a search for Christian internet filters, there are also general-market filters designed to monitor your children's internet activity. I know men who use these for themselves, even sharing them with accountability partners. As you know, websites and URLs tend to change frequently, but at this writing, here are some that remain active:

1. Net Nanny: known for its robust filtering and monitoring capabilities and offers content filtering, time management, and reporting.
2. Covenant Eyes: provides accountability and filtering services; sends reports to accountability partners.
3. Qustodio: a comprehensive parental control software that monitors and blocks explicit content.
4. Family Link by Google: a free app that allows parents to set digital ground rules.
5. K9 Web Protection: a free internet filter that helps block inappropriate content.
6. Circle: helps manage usage and content access.
7. Norton Family: a comprehensive control suite that includes web monitoring, time management, and location tracking.
8. Bark: primarily focused on online safety but also offers features for monitoring online activities.

What does this mean for your choice of movies to attend? Many include at least softcore porn and nudity. Do you wholly write off R-rated fare, or do you avert your eyes when necessary? Do you literally flee, leaving the theater when a sex scene or nudity is shown? I can't make those decisions for you, but prayerfully and honestly examine yourself and how such scenes affect you, and plant whatever hedges you need to protect your eyes, heart, mind, and marriage.

Regardless of the Cause . . .

A porn addiction may not have been the cause of Christopher's falling for Ashley in the previous chapter, but the resulting chaos was no less devastating. The second marriages that evolve out of situations like theirs seldom work. Make no mistake, however: Even if their new marriage had seemed idyllic, the entire situation still would have been disastrous for their previous spouses, Christopher's children, and both extended families.

First, both should have been aware of the potential danger and recognized the infatuation for what it was. This is basic, though not admitted by most Christians. It simply is not uncommon in the workplace to meet someone with whom there seems to be an immediate bonding. You like her, she likes you, you hit it off. That's the time to deal with the situation, because it can easily evolve into a serious dilemma.

You can be married ten years and still develop a crush on someone. You think about her, find yourself talking about her, quoting her (even to your spouse), and generally become enamored with her. Consult any survey results on this topic, and you'll find respondents overwhelmingly report that the major factor contributing to extramarital relationships is physical and emotional attraction, nearly doubling marital dissatisfaction.[6]

Second, recognizing the danger, both should have reminded themselves that this was nothing more than an adult version of adolescent puppy love, and it would pass. It really would. It always does if you don't feed the fantasy. The person is off-limits, and you should run from the situation as from a contagious disease.

You may still see the person in the work setting, and you may still enjoy proper interaction with her. But ground rules must be set. Never tell the person that you're attracted to her. Talk about your spouse frequently in front of her. Tell your spouse about the person, but use your own judgment about how fully to explain your dilemma.

I have a friend who seems to delight in telling his wife about all the women on whom he develops such instant and fleeting crushes. He encourages her to do the same. But while she admits she is susceptible to similar experiences, she prefers not to talk about them or to hear about his. My own wife is fully aware of my hedges, and thus she's not threatened by my extolling the appropriate virtues of a colleague. Of course, I don't rhapsodize about someone's looks or say stupid things like "If I had met her before I met you . . ."

When you first become aware of the impact the other person has on you, that's the time to move into action. You should be able to determine the extent of the danger a person represents to you by your own body language, how you sit or stand when talking with her, how much eye contact seems acceptable, whether you seem magnetized by her, and how much you look forward to seeing her.

Don't treat your new friend the way you would an old, respected friend. Refrain from touching her, being alone with her, flirting with her (even in jest), or saying anything to her you wouldn't say if your spouse, or hers if she's married, were there. (While you may not be so rigid in your conduct with a longtime friend of the opposite sex, beware. Certain guidelines must still be enforced. Friendships, especially with long-admired associates, can turn intimate even more quickly than new alliances.)

> If hedges are planted early enough, preferably well in advance of even meeting someone else, they can be painless and can nip marriage-threatening relationships before they get started.

So what could Christopher and Ashley have done? Had either realized they were becoming enamored with each other, they could have shifted gears, gone into a protective mode, and saved themselves from ruining many lives.

If hedges are planted early enough, preferably well in advance of even meeting someone else, they can be painless and can nip marriage-threatening relationships before they get started. That's why we so desperately need practical suggestions on how to plant impenetrable boundaries around our marriages.

The Size of the Problem

If you can believe the iconic *Hite Report on Male Sexuality*,[7] which I don't recommend reading or wholly believing, nearly three-fourths of married men cheat on their wives. Admittedly, the responses came from people with enough interest in the subject to answer a multi-page questionnaire that gave them the opportunity to discuss sex in the most pedestrian and vulgar terms, robbing it of any sacred mystery. In fact, the monumental report itself (1,129 pages in hardback) could be enlisted as a masturbatory aid, if one were so inclined. A huge percentage of the respondents were apparently so inclined, as evidenced in their comments.

On the subject of adultery, the author summarized: "The great majority of married men were not monogamous. Seventy-two percent of men married two years or more had had sex outside of marriage; the overwhelming majority did not tell their wives, at least at the time [of the incidents]."

Given the unscientific, nonrepresentative nature of the research, the above quotation can be taken with a healthy dose of salt, but it should be noted that a significant number of respondents referred to themselves as born-again Christians. Comparing this body of research with similar Christian surveys provides a rough idea of where believers fit in the overall scheme of marital faithfulness.

Twenty years ago, the *Barna Update* reported that a study of what Americans believed was moral and immoral revealed that nearly half the population thought that sex outside of marriage was okay.[8] Alarmingly, just two decades later, pollster Barna reported that 24 percent of Gen Z (those born between 1981 and 1996) "strongly agrees that what is morally right and wrong changes over time based on society."[9]

When a famous television evangelist announced he was stepping aside from his ministry because of an affair, I shook my head. I had never been a follower of the man, but I had been bemused by his apparently confused set of values. Sadly, the news of his moral failure was thus not a surprise. Further revelations included gross financial mismanagement, empire building, and even homosexuality.

Another Christian television personality's moral failure included a lifelong fascination with pornography and an apparent attempt to get as close as possible to extramarital sex without actually committing it.

Hearing of the ruined ministries of television evangelists or other respected Christian leaders due to sexual immorality is one thing. Seeing the same happen to your neighbor, your friend, or a family member is something else altogether. It may be hard to identify with the man who has everything—a ministry, wealth, status, popularity, a beautiful family—and risks it all for a season (or even just a moment) of pleasure, but it is not hard to identify with the man next door. Or in the mirror.

When your assistant pastor, brother-in-law, or best friend from college falls, that's too close to home. Then you get to see at close range the tumble of dominoes set in motion by infidelity.

3
THE PRICE

Infidelity. What a genteel word for what it describes. Such a word goes down easier than violating one's trust, breaking one's marriage vows, being unfaithful, sleeping around, fornicating, committing adultery. But using a mild word for sin doesn't change a thing.

I was twelve years old when I was first affected by the ravages of immorality. Something was wrong in the only church I had ever known, and no one would tell me what was going on. There were meetings, public and private; charges; accusations; arguments; tears; and factions. I badgered and bugged and bothered my mother until she told me what I later wished I didn't know.

"You're too young to deal with it," she said.

"No, I'm not, Mom. I'm twelve!" How old that sounded!

"You'll wish you hadn't asked."

"Just tell me! Please!"

"You won't believe it."

"Yes, I will! Tell me!"

"Would you believe me if I told you our pastor doesn't love his wife anymore?"

"No!"

"See?"

It couldn't be true. The pastor and his wife were perfect! They had four biological children and had adopted another. I had looked up to and admired them for as long as I could remember.

A young married woman in the church had been the center of the rumors. Was there an affair? Had someone seen them embrace? Could the stories be true of the pastor berating his wife? My head swam as the rumors flew.

The pastor's final sermon was a not-so-veiled admission of a mistake, but not adultery. He was confessing an error from years before—his choice of a wife. Even those who refused to believe the charges of adultery expressed horror over that public humiliation of his mate.

The church was ravaged by a near split soon after his departure. Then came the news of the divorce. That little church was left in pieces, and it took years for it to pull itself back together.

I was young and naïve enough to believe no such trauma had ever before hit a wonderful church like ours, nor could it ever happen again. Since then, sadly, I have heard countless such stories about pastors and have lived through more—including of both a senior pastor and an assistant pastor I sat under. One left notes for his trusted friends and associates praising God for "this new, divine love that is so wonderful that the Lord had to author it." Another friend tried to convince me that the relationship that broke up both his and his mistress's marriages was "in the center of God's will."

The Root

What seemed an aberration in a small town during my childhood was merely a harbinger of the marital devastation that plagues the Christian community today. At the beginning of this century, pollsters George Barna and Mark Hatch, in their book *Boiling Point: How Coming Cultural Shifts Will Change Your Life*, reported that one of four adults "who have ever been married has also experienced a divorce—and, amazingly, the incidence of divorce is slightly higher among born-again Christians than among others [27 percent versus 24 percent]."[1]

Of course, today, marriages break up at such alarming rates that it's hard to find someone who has not been affected by divorce in his or her immediate family. How many can you count in your own family, including grandparents on both sides, aunts, uncles, and your own siblings?

You may not know how many of those divorces were the result of immorality, but half is a fair assumption. Women leave their husbands for a variety of complex reasons, the most minor of which—according to marriage counselors—is their own lust. Rarely do you hear of a woman who simply fell for someone who, by his sexual appeal alone, turned her head and heart from her own husband.

But men—yes, even those who would blame their "frumpy, crabby, boring" wives for their own roving eyes—don't really need an excuse. They point to myriad reasons for having to leave, but it nearly always can be traced to lust, pride, and a false sense of their own strength.

My longtime friend Joni Eareckson Tada has written and spoken about this. She has said:

Some people find our Lord's approach to lust unnecessarily harsh. Jesus says, "If your right eye causes you to stumble, gouge it out and throw it away. . . . If your right hand causes you to stumble, cut it off and throw it away" (Matthew 5:29-30, NIV). He's not being literal here, but we get the idea. When it comes to lust, Jesus prescribes a severe, even radical operation.

In other words, this is nothing to coddle or play with—just as one would not play with a venomous snake. If we don't deal severely with lust, then a glance becomes a gaze. A thought becomes an action. A casual fantasy becomes heartbreak and a nightmare. So, yes, be harsh with such inclinations. Walk away. Avert your gaze. Leave the movie. Turn off your computer. These actions will result in God's blessing—and spare you years of regret.[2]

Justification

Think of the men you know and the reasons they gave for finding someone new. Did some have incredibly attractive, even sexy wives? Can all those men complain of their wives' frigidity? And even if they could, does this in any way excuse the breaking of their sacred vows?

My own experience in trying to counsel straying husbands reveals a strange bent. A man who has cheated on his wife often invents reasons after the fact. The man who once taught marriage seminars, raved about his wife, treated her right, and was proud of her must now say:

"We hid the truth. Our marriage was never good."
"In private, she was not what she appeared to be in public."
"I never really loved her."
"She didn't understand me." (The oldest saw in the toolkit.)

And one more that became my favorite excuse to hate:

"Actually, I disobeyed God by marrying her in the first place."

No Excuse

We've all heard the adage that every broken marriage has two sides and there's no such thing as a completely innocent party. However, those statements need examination. True, none of us knows what goes on behind closed doors, and we all know how base we can be in private compared to the image we like to project.

But if you know divorced couples, you know of examples where, even if the wife was not entirely innocent, she was certainly not guilty of anything that justified her husband's leaving her. I've been acquainted with enough such offending men to see their defenses coming a mile away. Suddenly this woman we all know as a wonderful person—not perfect, maybe harried and overworked, maybe not as dazzling as she was when they first married—is now painted as a monster. This from the man who is no prize himself and yet has justified breaking the laws of God, breaking his promises to his wife, violating their union, and blaming it on her!

A man who has cheated on his wife often invents reasons after the fact.

I once knew a denominational leader in his sixties who carried on a yearlong affair with a younger woman. When he was exposed and defrocked and called before his superiors, he brought along his wife, who took full responsibility. No confession from him. No apology. It was her fault, he said. She said it herself.

Call it what you will, but a man with as perfect a wife as he could ever want is still capable of lust, of a senseless seeking of that which would destroy him and his family. If he does not fear his own potential and plant a hedge around himself and his marriage, he's headed for disaster.

A Healthy Fear

Shall we all run scared?
Yes! Fear is essential.

"There are several good protections against temptation," Mark Twain said, "but the surest is cowardice."[3]

Look around. Let your guard down; don't remind yourself that you made a vow before God and men; don't set up barriers for your eyes, your mind, your hands, your emotions—and see how quickly you become a statistic.

A man may say, "It could never happen to me. I love my wife. We know each other inside and out. We've left the emotional infatuation stage that ruled our courtship and honeymoon, and we love God's way: unconditionally and by the act of our wills. We each know the other is not perfect, and we accept and love each other anyway. We're invulnerable to attack, especially by lust that leads to immorality." But when that man falls—because he has not planted hedges to protect himself—his tune changes. He makes excuses, saying he fell out of love, the old magic was gone, the wife got too busy with the house and kids, and his needs were not being fulfilled.

Worse, the Christian deserter becomes so infatuated with his new love that he often gives God the credit. Know a counseling pastor or a Christian psychologist? Ask him how many times he's heard a man say, "This new relationship is so beautiful that God has to be behind it." Never mind that it goes against all sense and every tenet of Scripture, not to mention everything the man has ever believed in and stood for.

A friend hit me with that excuse once, and I quickly moved farther away from him to another chair. He looked at me in surprise. "If God strikes you with lightning for that," I said, "I'd rather not be so close."

What Is Happening?

Okay, I'm an aging baby boomer. When I was in elementary school, I knew one, maybe two kids from broken homes. Divorce among church people was almost nonexistent. Now the solid, happy marriage is the exception. From people we never dreamed would have problems come stories of affairs, adultery, separation, and divorce.

Ever notice how many middle-aged people in your church seem to have unusually young families? The divorce stigma still exists, so many divorced and remarried people just move on to a new church and never mention that previous families—from both sides—were left behind. I'm not implying that people in this situation should not be welcomed and allowed to worship and rebuild their lives—just that there are likely many more such couples than we know of.

This is not the forum in which to debate the issue of divorce. Scripture is clear that God hates divorce (see Malachi 2:16), but opinions vary as to whether He forbids it altogether or allows it in only one or two circumstances and as to whether remarriage is allowed regardless of the reason for the divorce.

No matter where you stand on these issues, you must agree that no one marries intending or wanting to divorce. Some, no doubt, from the beginning consider divorce a convenient option and vow to stay together for as long "as we both shall love." But even the Christian with the most liberal position on divorce says and believes on his wedding day that he is pledging himself to his wife forever. He may later forget it or decide it was merely archaic formality, but there's no way around it. His vows were legal, sacred, and moral. When he commits adultery, he breaks his promise.

One of the most effective ways to deal with a friend trying to justify his adultery is to say, "Jacob, don't forget that I was there. I heard you say it. I heard you promise that you would take no one but Emma unto yourself for as long as you both shall live."

"Yeah, but—"

"You can 'yeah, but' all you want, but the fact is, you broke your promise."

"But she—"

"Regardless of what she did or didn't do, you broke your promise, didn't you?"

That can take the wind out of any sail made of excuses.

Run, Don't Walk

A complex litany of events takes place between the vows and the adultery. It behooves those of us who want to remain pure to examine those events, expose them for what they are, and either avoid letting them happen or avoid letting Satan use them to lure us into justifying our sin.

Once we have identified the temptations to which we're vulnerable, what will we do about them? Will we pray over them? Resolve to conquer them? Turn over new leaves? Ironically, the answer is easier than that. As I've said, according to one liberating bit of Scripture, we are not to win; not to gain the victory; not to succeed by the sheer force of our wills, our consciences, or our determination.

Flee also youthful lusts: but follow righteousness, faith, charity, peace, with them that call on the Lord out of a pure heart.

2 TIMOTHY 2:22, KJV

We are to run. To flee. To get out. To get away. Why? Does this admonition to flee somehow serve as an admission on God's part that He did not even equip us with the ability to subdue our natures in this area? The question is valid. Concerning adultery, in the Old Testament God tells us, "You shall not . . ." (Exodus 20:14), and in the New Testament He says that if we so much as look upon a woman to lust after her, we have already committed adultery with her in our hearts (see Matthew 5:28).

In other areas, God grants us victory. We can win over jealousy, a bad temper, greed, and even pride. We can train our consciences to avoid theft, bad-mouthing, and lying. But do you know any man who could avoid a peek at pornography if convinced no one would find out?

If you want your mind blown, check out the statistics for porn site visits during this current decade alone at https://sexualalpha .com/how-many-people-watch-porn-statistics. The top three porn sites see nearly six billion visits each month. That's 135,000 visits per minute. In one year, more than fourteen porn videos are watched per person on the planet.[4]

That you're not alone if you're so addicted neither justifies the sin nor makes you feel any better, does it? Clearly there are times when we are stronger than at other times. So what are we to do when temptation rages? If we are weak and have not taken precautions, if we have not applied preventive medicine, we have already failed. The only answer is to plan, to anticipate danger, to plot the escape.

The time to plant hedges is before the enemy attacks.

4

WHO IS AT FAULT?

Two of the most fascinating and misunderstood differences between men and women are in our thought processes and our sexual triggers. I was in the eighth grade when short skirts became popular. I thought I'd died and gone to heaven. Our school went through ninth grade, so to me, ninth-grade girls were women. Of course, back then what I considered short skirts were just an inch or two above the knee. Lord, have mercy! The trend would escalate to microminis by the time I reached college; so I spent my entire adolescence with my eyes open.

I suppose that era made me a leg man, though it would be a lie to say that any other female physical attribute is far down my appreciation list. Lest I sound like a wolf-whistling lecher, please know that this was a private sport. While we junior high boys might nudge another guy so he could follow our eyes to a choice target, for some reason we didn't admit to each other how deeply we felt about looking at girls.

Indeed, I thought I was probably the only Christian boy attracted to the female figure. From childhood on, I had read letters in a denominational magazine from teenagers lamenting having gone too far in their relationships and pleading for advice on how to control themselves. That turned out to be a good foundation for me when I began dating and facing temptation. I credit that early input—along with dating virtuous women—for my coming to my wedding night as virginal as my bride: wholly.

Yet in junior high and high school, I feared I would wind up as one of those letter writers. I was so enamored with women and their sensual beauty that I was convinced I had the potential to become a fiend. When I realized that even more exciting to me than any sports drama was watching a girl cross her legs and catching a glimpse of thigh, I knew I had it bad.

> I was so enamored with women and their sensual beauty that I was convinced I had the potential to become a fiend.

Had I only known this was normal! That I was not alone! That such attraction to women, yes, even to their sexuality, was God's idea! Is that heresy? It's not now, and it wasn't then. Though I can't recall having completely lustful thoughts in junior high, I carried a deep sense of guilt about even wanting to look at girls. As best I can recall, I had no thoughts of illicit sex. Still, I felt guilty. Something seemed wrong with thinking about this all the time. What a relief it would have been to discover that (depending on which expert you read) the typical American adolescent male thinks about sex no fewer than four times every minute!

Of course, as I graduated from puberty and went on for a master's degree in girl watching, it became more and more difficult to separate looking and appreciating from lusting. It was only a small comfort to me when I heard a Christian youth leader say that

99 percent of all heterosexual boys admit having a problem with lust and that the other one percent are liars. I was devout in my faith and knew right from wrong, yet I seemed to have no control, no resolve, no victory in this area. I regret not having had an adult perspective that would have allowed me to enjoy those years with wonder and without guilt.

With my own three sons, I allowed for the natural attraction to and preoccupation with females, and we talked about it rather than pretending there was something wrong with it. Naturally, I cautioned them about thoughts, and we discussed openly the priceless value of their goal to reach marriage without having fallen into sexual sin.

Beyond that, I didn't pretend that they should chastise themselves for appreciating a form designed by God to attract them. Without being crude, we discussed which girl in an ad or on a television program was most attractive and why. I admitted that women were still fun to look at, even at my ripe age. They probably got tired of my cautioning them to be careful about dwelling on the sexual and to simply admire, delight in, enjoy, and respect God's beautiful creativity.

Take Responsibility for Your Own Actions

With that input, however, I also tried to instill in my sons the reality that what they chose to dwell on mentally was on them and that they needed to own up to it. Sharing the following true story helped buttress that counsel, I hope.

I handed a piece of luggage to a baggage handler at O'Hare, but when he took it, I didn't let go quickly enough. The bag shifted, got away from both of us, and hit the floor on one of its corners. It fell open, and my photo and sound equipment rattled out across the corridor.

It wasn't his fault, but rather than apologizing to simply express his regret over my embarrassment and inconvenience, or even scrambling to help pick everything up and make sure it wasn't damaged (it wasn't), the man defended himself.

As I crawled around gathering up tapes and film and equipment, he spewed out his explanation. "I didn't do that! You held on too long!"

"No problem," I said. "My fault."

I confess I said that in the hope that he would join me and finish the task quickly. He did not.

"Yup, you held on too long," he repeated. "That wasn't me."

I was angrier at his refusal to accept any responsibility than at the ordeal of having to retrieve all my stuff. At least it wasn't underwear.

I didn't say it was his fault, and I didn't need him to say it was his fault. We two had mishandled something. Surely each of us had had enough experience handing heavy items to another person. The deliverer has a responsibility to release the item once he has passed it on. The receiver has a responsibility to not turn away with such an item until he is sure he alone has it. Was it really important who contributed most to the mishap?

Passing blame has to be one of our earliest and basest defense mechanisms.

I was nearly finished when a woman behind the counter noticed and hurried to my aid. "I'm so sorry this happened," she said, as if she had done it herself. We both knew she had nothing to do with it, so clearly, she was simply expressing sympathy. She was sorry for me, not for herself.

She gave her coworker a look, as if expecting him to say or do something. All he did was repeat, "I didn't do that. He held on too long."

Her smile froze. "No one says you did it, and no one cares. We're just sorry it happened, aren't we? And aren't we eager to help straighten it out?"

By then, she and I were done. That man still didn't take the hint or even pretend to share responsibility, so I could only imagine how he reacts when something *is* his fault.

Passing blame has to be one of our earliest and basest defense mechanisms. Where do we learn to distance ourselves from blame so early? "It wasn't me—it was him!" "I didn't do it—she did!" "Don't blame me!" "It's not my fault!" Even Adam said, "It was the woman you gave me!" (see Genesis 3:12).

"Well, I woulda brought my book home, but the coach didn't give us enough time to go back to our lockers and . . ."

"She made me forget."

"He wouldn't lend me a pencil."

"No one knew what time it was."

"I didn't know you were here."

But that kind of talk doesn't end when childhood ends.

"Why didn't the magazine get published on time?"

"We didn't get the pages to the printer on time."

"Why?"

"Because the editors didn't get their corrections to the production manager in time."

"Why?"

"Because one was sick, and the others had to cover for him, and they got behind."

"Why didn't they find help or work overtime?"

"They didn't know whether anyone was available."

"Why didn't they ask their superiors?"

"Because they didn't think their superiors would do that kind of work."

"Why didn't the superiors make it clear in advance that they would help out in such emergencies?"

Will someone stop here and take personal responsibility for *something*? People pass and pass and pass the buck and then see it passed right back. Supervisors can go months without once hearing someone say, "That was my fault. I messed up. I forgot. I'll make it right."

In most cases, at least with me, blame shifting is really lying. I may have told myself it wasn't, but when I think back and really study the individual cases, I was pretending to be a victim of someone else's foul-up.

Oh, they may have really messed up, and I may truly have been a victim. But the responsibility had been mine, and thus I should have foreseen problems or been prepared to deal with them. Rather than rectify a situation, I claimed the alibi of someone else's failure and focused the attention there. I didn't sleep as well then as I do now.

What does all this have to do with maintaining fidelity in marriage? Stay with me.

I wish I could remember the first time in the business world that I simply took the blame, admitted my mistake, and set about righting it. I do recall that once I started doing that, I began to be looked at differently by my superiors. They saw me as a responsible person, honest, eager to do things right. I didn't waste time trying to assess blame and point fingers. I even took some blame that wasn't wholly mine. I knew if I studied the problem long enough, I could find a place where I had let down, had quit staying on top of something, and could have had something to do with the failure.

My point is that taking responsibility is first a mindset, and the more vigorously you cultivate it, the stronger you'll be when you make a mistake at home. Take the blame, fix the problem, and live with a clear conscience.

At a high-level meeting of VIPs, a friend of mine was responsible for asking the proper department to provide a mobile rack for the attendees' coats. He sent through the paperwork, received a signed receipt, noted that the proper date and location were designated, and relaxed. On the night of the meeting, he greeted the VIPs in the lobby, introduced his boss, and slipped out to be sure the dining room and meal were ready and the coat rack in place.

When he got downstairs, he walked past where the rack should have been, checked with the food service staff, and found all that in order. He then shot a double take at the empty space by the wall. No rack. And here came footsteps on the stairs.

He ran to the department that was supposed to have provided the rack. The area was dark. He peered through the glass, shielding outside light with his hands. Three coat racks were available behind the locked door. He hollered for a maintenance man, and one appeared at the end of the hall, looking at him, puzzled. "I need to get in here!" my friend said.

"I can't let you do that," the man said.

"You have a master key, don't you?"

"Yes, sir, but I can't—"

My friend ran toward him. They knew each other, so there was no threat. "The president needs a coat rack for the VIPs, and it's my responsibility."

"Did you requisition one?"

"Of course, but—"

"Then you did your job. Somebody else messed up."

"I'm not interested in that. Open this door, and I'll take the heat."

"I'll let you unlock it, but I'm not going to."

"Fair enough," my friend said, bouncing on his toes to get the maintenance man to hurry. Seconds later he was flying down the hall toward the dining room, pushing the rack. He whirled into sight just as the VIPs arrived. He stopped, took a deep breath, and tucked in his shirt. "Right here, folks," he said, gliding into position. "May I take your coats?"

The president never noticed how close they came to having a little faux pas. My friend's excuses and an explanation of how he had done his part would have been irrelevant. Paper trails wouldn't cut it. He had been given the responsibility to provide the coat rack, and he had done it. Had he not done it, it would have been his fault. Someone else let him down, but he would have had to take the full blame.

I would love to tell you that the department in charge apologized to him for the inconvenience, but—you guessed it—a shifting of the blame began. There had been an emergency, a new employee, an earlier quitting time, a misunderstanding.

All that to say, if you're asked to do something and you're counting on six other suppliers to make it happen, take responsibility. See that it gets done. Stay on top of it. People don't want excuses. They want performance.

And when something does go wrong, even if it's not your fault, express sorrow for the inconvenience and make it right. Too often you could have done something to prevent the problem, so accept the blame, too.

This carries over to your marriage as well. Be prepared to accept responsibility for your own actions and you'll find yourself more vigilant about even your wedding vows.

5

DISTINCTIVE VIEWS
OF INTIMACY

What do you tell your kids about sex? Decades ago, Drs. Miriam and Otto Ehrenberg classified parents into four categories according to their views of how to teach children about sex:

- *Sex Repressive*: Sex is bad and should be discussed or dealt with only in that light.
- *Sex Avoidant*: Sex is okay but is best not talked about.
- *Sex Obsessive*: Sex is everything; no taboos; even young children should be conversant about it.
- *Sex Expressive*: Sex is good and healthy and should be discussed appropriately.

In their book *The Intimate Circle*, they wrote:

> The aim of Sex Repressive parents is very specific: to curb sexual behavior and keep their children, especially

their daughters, away from sexual entanglements before they are married. The impact of Sex Repressive parents, however, goes way beyond this goal. They instill a sense of shame in children about their innate sexuality which alienates children from their parents and interferes with their later capacity to form satisfying relationships with the opposite sex. . . .

Children in these circumstances grow up feeling bad about the sexual stirrings which are an essential part of their nature, and resentful towards their parents for disapproving of this very basic aspect of their being.[1]

All this time later, well into the twenty-first century, any conscientious parent would want to be Sex Expressive. But for Christians, there's a major problem with this secular view. While it's almost always positive and healthy to be Sex Expressive, we must also instill in our children the biblical admonition that sex before or outside of marriage is wrong, is sin, and has consequences. In other words, during the time of our children's peak sexual awareness—adolescence—we might be labeled Sex Repressive by the experts, even though we assure our children that sex is good and healthy and fun and is, in fact, God's idea.

I know some people may laugh at my notion of looking at women to appreciate God's creativity and would accuse me of inventing a spiritual reason to leer. I maintain that after years of steeling myself to avert my eyes from something made attractive by God, developing an appreciation for it is far healthier. Clearly it would be wrong to gawk at and dwell upon some stranger's beauty, especially when I have vowed before God and man to put my wife ahead of all others. Dianna knows that I'm attracted to pretty women (she is one, after all). She also knows that I know they are off-limits and that even entertaining a lustful thought is wrong.

The point is, I don't pretend before my wife that I no longer look at other women. My gaze doesn't linger and my thoughts stay in check (not easily and not always), but how much worse it would be if I pretended to have been blind since our wedding and she caught me sneaking a peek. Her standard line is "When he quits looking, he quits cooking."

Don't get the idea that my eyes are always roving and that my poor wife can't keep my attention. (Anyone who has seen her knows otherwise.) It doesn't take a lingering look to appreciate beauty, and there are more than enough reasons not to stare at other women. First, it would threaten Dianna and jeopardize my covenant with her. Second, it would be dangerous to my thought life, because past a casual observance of God's handiwork (go ahead, laugh!), my eyes and mind have no right to dwell there. Even if the woman isn't in a relationship with anyone else, I belong to Dianna!

We must also instill in our children the biblical admonition that sex before or outside of marriage is wrong, is sin, and has consequences.

It's interesting to note the double standard that comes into play here. My glance at a nice-looking woman is even quicker when she's escorted. I know how I feel when men stare at my wife. I watch their eyes. I'm possessive and jealous. I have a right to be. If their gaze lingers, I assume they're trying to catch her eye, and they probably are. No fair. Out of bounds. Off-limits. She's mine.

It gives me a great sense of security that Dianna is largely unaware of how many heads she turns and that, even if she were aware, she's not one to return another man's gaze. Still, I resent it when I see someone stare at her, and I want to practice the Golden Rule when the shoe is on the other foot.

I was always quick to point out to my sons that the rush of feeling they might experience for a beautiful woman should never be mistaken for true love. Such a rush is mere infatuation, physical and sensual attraction, a path to a dead end. A relationship may begin with physical attraction—and of course it's a bonus to be sexually attracted to your spouse—but to build an entire relationship on that alone leads to disaster. It's also important to differentiate here between true beauty and cheap sexuality. Almost any woman—within reason—can dress or make herself up in such a way that she looks sexy and available. I maintain that unless a man is looking for thrills, he won't find such a creature attractive. Focusing on an escort-type is selfish and fleshly, perverting the natural attraction between the sexes that was God's idea.

Women may shake their heads in disgust at my obviously male perspective. Guilty. I was born this way. I have women friends who cover much the same territory from the female viewpoint in their own excellent books, but we couldn't have written each other's books. Men and women think and act differently and *are* different, and no amount of modern talk can convince me otherwise.

A high school youth leader first taught me that girls don't think at all the way guys do. I didn't believe him at first. Even the minor exposure to pornography I'd experienced as a sheltered, young, evangelical male told me that women could be easy and flirty, come-ons, you name it. Therefore, I assumed that innocent, young Christian girls who dressed, acted, walked, or talked provocatively knew exactly what they were doing. Unless the girls were asking for trouble, which I found difficult to accept, they were playing a dangerous and contemptuous game with us guys. They knew we are turned on by hair-trigger switches through the mind and all five senses; so, unless they meant business, they were being cruel.

This idea that they were actually, on the whole, ignorant of their effect or unaware how males react was so revelatory and revolutionary that I couldn't accept it. I'm not saying there weren't or aren't women who may fit precisely the description in the above paragraph, but just that most of those who turn men on would be shocked to know how they are viewed.

I put that theory to the test as a high school senior and a college freshman. I dated a Christian girl who was careful and virtuous and could not be described as a flirt. I discussed with her the actions and dress of mutual friends and found that she agreed with our youth leader. The girls in question were ignorant or naïve. They were not sinister or on the prowl. I mustered my courage and began to ask them.

My freshman year at a Christian college allowed me to meet many beautiful female students—a whole range of personalities, modes of dress, and behavior. This was back when rainbows were only objects in the sky, so our school policy stipulated that skirts could be no shorter than the top of the knee. Some of my best friends, women I respected and admired and enjoyed looking at, seemed to push the rule to the limit. How does one determine the top of the knee? (My friends and I volunteered to help!) Depending on the skirt, the material, and the woman, a skirt that was legal while she was standing might be four inches above the knee when she sat. Even the most modest skirt that touched the top of the knee was a problem for men when a woman wanted to cross her legs.

Not wanting to appear an oddball, I would wait until I considered a woman my friend before I broached the subject of whether women knew how their attire affected men. "Can I ask you something, just out of curiosity?"

"Sure."

"How would you feel if you thought that the way you dressed caused men to lust?"

I asked at least six college women, ages ranging from eighteen to twenty-one. Every one of them responded with some variation of "Oh, I'm sure we don't have any guys that perverted around here."

Remember, I was not on a crusade to get the rule changed or even to get the skirts lengthened. I was just testing a theory, and I was stunned by the response. They actually didn't know. They dressed for fashion, for comfort, and for their own taste. Some even admitted they dressed to impress their women friends—ones whose fashion sense intrigued them. Had they realized they were causing problems for male students, I have no doubt they'd have made adjustments.

As you might imagine, things have mightily changed in the ensuing decades. A Christian college newspaper recently carried an editorial by a woman student who said she and her sisters had gotten the point. They felt a responsibility not to lead their brothers in Christ into sin. She took it a step further and said that some of the guys could take a lesson in how to wear their jeans.

That's a relatively new concept: men turning women on by what they wear and how they wear it. What has contributed to this shift? Some would say novels—written by men that portray women triggered sexually by the same stimuli that affect men, plus the popularity of male strippers and even some magazines that depict male nudity—not to mention today's hookup culture. It is generally accepted that women are aroused by environment, atmosphere, tenderness, romance, and touch. The idea of men baring themselves used to be considered repulsive to women.

Today, however, you can even see television commercials in which girls on the beach rate the various body parts of the men who walk by. But women friends and relatives tell me that while the occasional broad shoulder or narrow hip might be a mild turn-on, most women are still not sexually aroused in the same way men are. There is no longer any question that women can be aroused to a similar state of excitement and eroticism, but the route is different.

These differences in attraction actually compete with each other. A man is turned on by the mere thought of a beautiful woman—imagining, fantasizing about the possibilities. When he meets a woman, the scenario has already been played out in his mind. She might like his voice, his smile, his manner. Meanwhile, he's lightyears ahead. She smiles at his interest. Then he says or does something inappropriate. Immediate disaster. She's turned off, he's offended, and neither understands what went wrong. She thinks he's a typical male. He thinks she's a typical female. Both are right.

Some like to blame God for this seeming inequity. ("I can't help myself; He made me this way.") Others say our makeup justifies aggressiveness, that men are to be the leaders, planners, visionaries. Women are to be submissive, supportive, reactive.

Neither view is wholly acceptable, of course, and in this century, we're seeing a raft of new ideas changing how the differences between the genders and their respective responsibilities were once commonly explained. In an opinion piece titled "In Search of Non-Toxic Male Sexuality" in the June 12, 2023, issue of *Christianity Today* magazine, Zachary Wagner (editorial director for the Center for Pastor Theologians) posed the question of whether we "can recover a healthy, Christ-honoring vision for masculinity."[2]

He made the case that while evangelicals have invested a colossal amount of energy into promoting "sexual purity" and a "biblical" vision for sexuality, the root problem remains. He said that "the pattern of scandal, abuse, and misconduct by men and male leaders makes clear that the purity movement has not solved the problem of unhealthy sexuality in the church." His point was that unhealthy representations of the movement have "perpetuated a hypersexual vision of masculinity. These scandals and patterns of dehumanization have infected the church, not despite the purity movement but in many ways because of it."

How can this be? What's been the problem with certain aspects of the so-called purity movement? Wagner posited that it's "time to change the way we talk and think about male sexuality. This sub-Christian view of masculinity creates a culture in which men are allowed to wallow in ongoing sexual immaturity."

Wagner said that the church is

beginning to grasp how purity culture objectifies women and dehumanizes them. What's often less appreciated is the way the movement also has dehumanized *men*. If purity culture dehumanized women by treating them as sexual objects, it dehumanized men by casting them as sexual animals. If it hypersexualized women's bodies, it hypersexualized men's minds. Much of our rhetoric and resources adopted the culture's assumption that men are helplessly and hopelessly hypersexual, a belief perpetuated in TV sitcoms and accepted in "locker-room talk." . . .

In a bizarre twist on the prosperity gospel, some Christian teachers have argued that following God's design for sex is the path to your best sex life. Wives are charged to be more sexually available to their husbands as the solution to their struggles with pornography. Single men are told that God's "provision" for their out-of-control sexual desires is marriage, reducing a covenant relationship to a permissible sexual outlet. Since sexual satisfaction subtly becomes normalized as the rightful inheritance of godly men, certain forms of male sexual entitlement are all too common.

He concluded that "We can aspire to more for men. Not just to stop lashing out in violence or sinking into compulsive sexual behavior, but to become more truly human as advocates for justice, faithful friends, noble protectors, honorable husbands, and selfless lovers. As we look to Christ, the true man, we can become new men."

Ironically, Rachel Joy Welcher had covered much of the same ground nearly two years earlier, also in *Christianity Today* (October 14, 2021).[3] The author of *Talking Back to Purity Culture: Rediscovering Faithful Christian Sexuality* wrote:

I remember believing that men truly couldn't control their lust if women didn't take on the responsibility of dressing and acting in ways that squelched it. These books made it clear to me that the responsibility for sexual sin and temptation—even assault—fell squarely on the shoulders of women. I couldn't believe some of the lies I saw sandwiched in between Bible verses or the tactics that were used and the carrots that were dangled.

Is it possible all of us—men and women alike—unthinkingly bought into the purity culture that advised women to be submissive to men who were simply wired this way? Does that not further sexualize wives and exonerate husbands who treat them as objects of desire to "help" them remain faithful?

Sure, there are times, especially as teenagers, when we men might wish we hadn't been equipped with an engine that idles like a rocket but isn't supposed to be launched for years. But to hide behind nature to justify aggression and chauvinism is cowardly. Theologians and psychologists can work out the reasons we're made this way. Our task is to channel our drives into something positive, plant hedges around our marriages, and glorify God in the process.

> There are times, especially as teenagers, when we men might wish we hadn't been equipped with an engine that idles like a rocket but isn't supposed to be launched for years.

6

WHAT'S IN A LOOK?

Flirting is fun and usually begins in innocence. It's a hard habit to break, even after marriage. Yet it causes jealousy. Worse, it puts us into situations we never intended to fall into, and it creates misunderstandings that can lead to infidelity.

Apart from sex, what could be more fun than flirting? If you say softball, you're reading the wrong book.

Flirting is so much fun because the rushes, emotions, and pleasures are sexual. It's foreplay with no payoff. It makes the heart race, the face flush, and a feeling of well-being wash over the body. It seems harmless, but it's not. It may seem even more harmless when it's over the internet, perhaps in direct messages (DMs) with an old girlfriend you found on Facebook or Instagram. But again, it's not.

If you want to flirt, flirt with your wife. She may not look, feel, or sound the way she did when you first flirted with her years ago, but she still wants you to flirt with her. Try it. Wink at her across the room. Blow her a kiss no one else sees. Play footsie with her under the table. Give her a squeeze, a pinch, a tickle no one else notices.

Apart from sex, what could be more fun than flirting? If you say softball, you're reading the wrong book.

Are you afraid she'll think you're crazy? Well, you are crazy, aren't you? Put yourself in her place. Would you like to be flirted with by someone who loves you, someone who can tease about what she might do with you later and then deliver? Do you, or would you, appreciate your wife making a pass at you, making a suggestive comment, giving you a knowing look? I do, and she does, and I love it.

Married couples do not commonly flirt with each other, and the practice may have to be relearned. Marital flirting is really no different from adolescent flirting. You can do the same things, only everything you're thinking about and hoping will happen is legal, normal, acceptable, and beautiful. Marital flirting is fun and safe.

But . . . who do we usually flirt with? Who would we like to flirt with? Good friends from work? From church? Young people? Wives of friends?

We don't mean anything by it. It's innocent. They're safe. It's a way of having a good time at no one else's expense.

Right?

Then why does it bother us so much when we detect someone trying to flirt with our wives? A wink; a smile; a "Hey, why don't you dump this guy and run off with me? Haha"; a touch; and the hair on our necks bristles. *Who does this guy think he is? He thinks this is funny?*

We're also extremely interested in how our wives react to such an approach. Can she bob and weave with the best of them, return the barbs, keep it alive? We trust her. She's faithful. It's all a game, a diversion.

Then why does it bother us so much?

Because the flirter has no right to the emotions, the inappropriate attention, the sexual/recreational lives of our spouses. I don't flirt with other women, even in jest, because I wouldn't want my wife to be offended or hurt or wonder or be embarrassed. And I certainly would not want her to do the same to me.

My wife doesn't flirt because something deep within her knows it is basically wrong. She doesn't have to fight the urge, and when someone tries to flirt with her, her unpracticed reactions cool his heels. She doesn't try to be mean or cold—though she could be if someone actually came on to her—but extramarital flirtation is so far from her modus operandi that she usually doesn't recognize it. Thus, her reaction is either puzzlement or seriousness, and a flirt needs a target who flexes, who gives, who responds.

Because I enjoy having fun and being funny, and because my mind tends to find humor in words and unusual combinations of ideas, I could easily flirt with anyone I thought was receptive. Flirting can be humorous. If someone says something flirtatious to me, my first impulse is to expand on it, play with it, and see how quick and funny I can be. But I resist that. It isn't fair. It's mental and emotional unfaithfulness. I would be exercising a portion of my brain and soul reserved for my exclusive lover.

I know that seems rigid, so I am careful not to chastise, put down, or otherwise embarrass or insult a woman who might flatter me by flirting with me. It is flattering, of course, even if it does somehow lower my esteem for her. I usually respond with humor that changes the subject or ends the conversation, in the hope that she will later realize I deflected the approach without embarrassing her.

The reason I don't scowl at flirters or lecture them is that I believe most flirting is well intentioned. It's meant to be a compliment, a friendly gesture, a you-and-me kind of thing that separates those of us with certain kinds of minds and attitudes from everyone else in the room. It's elitist. It's subtle. It marks us as smart and clever.

But, as usual, we find ourselves confronted by the age-old difference between men and women. A friend of mine, a woman, says something grossly inappropriate to me almost every time I see her. She does it to bug me, and she has absolutely no ulterior motives. Even my wife thinks she's a scream.

I believe women mean something entirely different by flirting from what men do. Most women I have discussed this with tell me that they agree that flirting with someone else's husband is not right, and often they feel guilty later. But initiating the flirting or responding to someone else's approach is fun and exciting because of the attention.

"Usually it surprises me," a friend says. "Often a meeting of the eyes or a smile or a flirtatious joke makes me realize for the first time that a man is even aware of me in a group. Then, I admit, I encourage it, but with no thought of actually leading him on."

I'm not saying that men intend anything serious at first either, but if a flirtatious advance is returned, it tends to escalate. I know two men who have left their wives for other men's wives, and it all began with what each party thought was harmless flirting.

In one case, the process took a year; in the other, only a little over a month. In both cases, the same thing happened. The man started it. The woman responded. They teased each other on several occasions until the man grew bold enough to think that maybe she meant something by her encouraging responses. In the first case, he made a move on her; she was stunned and hurt; and in the apologizing and reconciling process, they fell in love. In the second, the woman was surprised but pleased at the man's interest, and in the throes of a bad marriage she jumped ship, and two marriages sank.

As with many other innocent activities that eventually get out of hand, flirting can be a good and natural part of a progression toward true love. God made us able to respond emotionally and physically to attention from the opposite sex, and that is the initial aim of flirting. But like any of His gifts, this one can be cheapened and counterfeited and used for evil as well as for good.

Youthful Flirting

I was twelve when I first experienced the euphoric surge of excitement at knowing that a girl and I had locked eyes on purpose. What began as an accident became an anticipated activity. What a revelation! It happened like this.

I helped a friend deliver papers every day. We traded off, from one day to the next, handling the two halves of the territory. One day I tossed a paper onto the big front porch of a house and then moved on. I had just dropped that paper on the steps when I heard the door open and saw a girl about my age come out to retrieve it.

I recognized her from school, though I didn't know her—not even her name. She was probably a year ahead of me. As she bent to pick up the paper, her long, brown hair cascaded over her face. When she stood up, she flipped it back into place with a turn of her head. And she looked right at me.

I had been idly watching her as I moved along, but I was embarrassed that she saw me, so I quickly looked elsewhere. But what was that out of the corner of my eye? Had I turned too quickly? Had she smiled at me? I shot a fast double take her way; she had already turned toward the door. But she must have seen me looking back at her, so she turned back.

We smiled shyly at each other and said nothing. I didn't know what she was thinking. Probably nothing. To a twelve-year-old, a thirteen-year-old is almost an adult, and I was very much on the young side of twelve. I probably had a ball glove in my newspaper bag, maybe even a pocketful of marbles. My hair would have been flying.

She was more sophisticated. Grown-up. She was probably just smiling at some dumb paperboy, I decided, but I sure liked it.

The next day, I pleaded with my friend to let me deliver on the same end of the route again. Nothing doing. I would have to wait another twenty-four hours to see that smile. I never considered that it was probably a fluke. Why hadn't I ever seen her before? Did I think she would wait at the window for me next time?

Two days later my hair was combed, my cleanest jeans were on, and I wore new tennies. I imagined her watching from halfway down the block. So I did my best to look older, more conscientious, important, in a hurry, doing a good job. A couple of times I walked past a house without dropping a paper, only to nonchalantly flip one behind my back to the precise spot. I was hot.

At the house before hers, I had to mount the steps and put the paper in the rungs under the mailbox. I casually bounded up the stairs two at a time, slipped the paper in, and jumped all the way to the ground. No problem. Thank goodness I didn't wind up with a face full of dirt. I imagined her watching, smiling, and I felt as if I could do anything. Down deep, I was hoping against hope she would come out to get the paper again.

I approached her porch. Slowly. Dropped the paper in front of the door. Turned. More slowly. Then moved resolutely to the next house. No action. No movement. No noise. I looked back several times, hoping. Nothing. Maybe that's why I was doing only one side of the street at a time. When I crossed at the corner and delivered papers to the other side of the same street, I could see her porch for half a block. I worked ever so deliberately.

The house directly across from hers was not that of a paper subscriber, but it sat on a wide expanse of lawn. I delivered the paper to the house before it, then traversed the entire distance to the next with my head turned, staring at the magic porch. Had someone planted a tree in my path the day before, I'd have worn it home. The trail I blazed was as circuitous as you can imagine for one who didn't have his eye on where he was going.

But my persistence paid off. She appeared. And she wore a fluffy, red dress. She stepped out, picked up the paper, went to the edge of the porch, leaned on the railing, and smiled at me. Her smile and her eyes followed me until I had to look away or careen into the street. This had been no accident. Could she have dressed up just for me? I couldn't swear to it, but clearly she had looked for me, smiled at me, and made it obvious she was pleased to have done so. I began wondering where we might raise our family.

You can't imagine the thrill unless you remember similar experiences on the threshold of puberty. We continued that ritual every other day for over a week—until I found out she was doing the same with my friend, the other delivery boy. I hadn't even said hello to my intended, and she had already cheated on me. I wasn't even motivated to fight for her. My interest cooled overnight.

As a freshman in high school, I enjoyed another silent flirting season with a girl in my algebra class. She was a fresh-faced blonde with glasses and a turned-up nose, and for some reason I loved to look at her. We sat on opposite sides of the room. To see her, I had to lean back and look past all the heads in my row. One day she caught me looking, so I turned back. But when I sneaked another peek, she was staring right at me.

My heart skipped. Was it obvious to everyone that we were in love? I didn't even know her name. Yet my pulse quickened, and I was short of breath when I caught her gaze as I leaned back and she leaned forward. We didn't even smile at each other. This was too intense. Occasionally I tried to tell myself I was imagining it, and then we would settle into our desks, the teacher would begin, and I would zero in on that pair of eyes.

For a week we stared at each other, sometimes for twenty minutes at a time. I was stunned the teacher didn't notice and call us on it. He would not have been able to see both of us staring at the same time, but he could have followed one's gaze to the other.

One day, when I had finally learned her name, I mustered the courage to send a note across to her. Everybody looked at her and then at me as she read it. "See you after class?" it read. She looked up at me, still unsmiling, and nodded. Has there ever been a longer forty-minute wait? I couldn't even look at her that day. I just studied the clock.

After class she went out the door, turned right, stood with her back against the wall and her books embraced in front of her, and waited expectantly. "Hi," I said.

"Hi," she said.

I wanted so badly to say something cool, such as, "You know, I've really enjoyed studying you these last several days, and I thought it was time we got better acquainted."

But I didn't. I said, "Um, I was wonderin' if you wouldn't mind if I walked you to your next class."

"No problem," she said in a voice too hard, too sharp for such a pretty face, "except it's like right here." She nodded to the study hall next to the algebra room.

"Oh, yeah, well, I guess you can make it there by yourself all right."

"Yeah," she said and walked away.

I saw her again, but I never looked at her, if you know what I mean. I was learning valuable lessons in illusion versus reality.

Flirting Today

My point is that the same surge of ecstasy is still available to me—or to any man—today. If you work at it, you can catch a woman's eye and see if she wants to play the game. The problem is that it's short of adultery only in the physical sense, and it can lead to that.

I'm sometimes embarrassed in public, maybe in a restaurant, when I happen to catch the gaze of a woman, look away, and then we look back at the same moment. Neither of us is looking for anything; each is embarrassed and wonders what the other thinks. I usually smile apologetically and then fight the urge to look once more.

I'm not looking for other women's eyes, though, and I don't want them or anyone, especially my wife, to think I am. There's a comfort, a sensuality, a sexuality, a bonding stronger than with anyone else when I look deeply into Dianna's eyes. I know her, I can read her, and we can communicate that way.

On the occasion of his and Ruth's sixtieth wedding anniversary, Dr. Billy Graham told me, "We realize that at this stage of our lives [in their mideighties and failing physically], we can continue our lifetime love affair with our eyes."

Besides looking, I also flirt with Dianna by touching, caressing, yes, even playing footsie. We consider these fun and funny personal and private ways of communicating. They make up a part of our sexual language of love, and every one of them—the looks, smiles, and suggestive comments—are off-limits for anyone else.

I don't flirt with anyone but my wife, and vice versa.

You flirt with your wife, and I'll flirt with mine.

7

IS THIS SCRIPTURAL?

People will tell you to beware of legalism, even in the area of sexual purity. True, a balanced, appropriate view makes our stand attractive rather than shrill. But Scripture is clear: There's a price for adultery.

We're far enough along now that the following should be no revelation: I'm assuming you care what God thinks about your life. If you don't, you're reading the wrong book. I believe in God, and I accept the Bible as the basis of authority for my life. If you don't, this has all long since appeared foolish to you anyway.

Perhaps you find yourself conflicted on these issues. Maybe you aren't sure about a personal God and are unsure whether the Bible is at all relevant. That puts you in the same category, sadly, as many who call themselves Christians. They are smorgasbord church people who sample what looks good and leave what doesn't. A God who cares about sexual conduct and even has rules regarding it doesn't fit the twenty-first century me-first society.

The problem with that view is that it assumes that God has rules for rules' sake. He's just a spoilsport, trying to make a Goody Two-shoes out of everybody. If we can't find practical reasons for following His rules, we justify ignoring them.

My simple mind cries out for a God who is personal, orderly, and logical. I believe that a God who created everything and loved us enough to make the supreme sacrifice for us has reasons for His prohibitions and would rather see us happy and fulfilled than miserable and confined.

There must be sense and logic behind His rules. Let's look at them briefly to determine what they are, and then let me make an amateur's—or at least a layman's—attempt at making them fit with my view of God as a fulfiller, not a taskmaster.

Here Comes the Judge

Jesus talked about the law most extensively in Matthew 5:17-19:

> Do not think that I came to destroy the Law or the Prophets. I did not come to destroy but to fulfill. For assuredly, I say to you, till heaven and earth pass away, one jot or one tittle will by no means pass from the law till all is fulfilled. Whoever therefore breaks one of the least of these commandments, and teaches men so, shall be called least in the kingdom of heaven; but whoever does and teaches them, he shall be called great in the kingdom of heaven.

The law He was talking about, of course, contains the Ten Commandments. Most people, even nonchurchgoers, can remember a few of these: Don't lie; don't murder; don't commit adultery; don't steal. We can see the obvious problems with lying, stealing, and murdering, but if sex is so good and beautiful and fun, what's wrong with a little adultery among friends? And what was Jesus talking about when He said He was fulfilling, not replacing, the law? This is the wrong forum in which to get into Jesus' claims of deity, but suffice it to say He was establishing Himself as one with God, the Son of God, the ful-fillment of God's law. The embodi-

I believe that a God who created everything and loved us enough to make the supreme sacrifice for us has reasons for His prohibitions and would rather see us happy and fulfilled than miserable and confined.

ment of perfection, the personification of sinlessness—that is Jesus Christ. Now—lest anyone else claim to also qualify as the righteous King—Jesus, in essence, changed all the rules.

Later in the same discourse He said:

> Unless your righteousness exceeds the righteousness of the scribes and Pharisees, you will by no means enter the kingdom of heaven. You have heard that it was said to those of old, "You shall not murder, and whoever murders will be in danger of the judgment." But I say to you that whoever is angry with his brother without a cause shall be in danger of the judgment.
>
> MATTHEW 5:20-22

Murder is worthy of judgment, but now even anger with a brother is just as bad. Who can live up to that standard? Only Jesus. Then He got down to the toughest part. "You have heard that it was said to those of old, 'You shall not commit adultery.' But I say to you that whoever looks at a woman to lust for her has already commit-ted adultery with her in his heart" (Matthew 5:27-28).

What's the point of all that? Wasn't the original law hard enough? Wasn't it a good enough standard by which to be judged? Why would Jesus rewrite it to make it impossible? Let me speculate, as a layman. Jesus, the God-man who died for us, could take no pleasure in making life difficult or unachievable for us. Clearly, He was setting a standard to make a point—that if someone was somehow able to keep from lying, murdering, and even coveting for an entire lifetime, there would still be no way to ever dream of following this new standard. If hatred and anger equal murder, and lust is adultery, we're all guilty.

Only Jesus could meet that standard; so we are forced to rely upon Him for our standing before God. He takes the penalty for our sin; He becomes our advocate before a holy God. God looks at us and sees not our sin but the perfection of Jesus, and we who would otherwise be unqualified to be in His presence are assured of a place with Him for eternity. The apostle Paul said it this way in 2 Corinthians 5:21: "For He made Him who knew no sin to be sin for us, that we might become the righteousness of God in Him."

Between Our Ears

When my friend Robert Wolgemuth teaches from Matthew, he makes the point that Jesus was not really talking about murder or adultery but about attitudes, what goes on between our ears. Jesus was talking about the things most people can't see. He was saying that the law is not about something you do or don't do; it's about who you are.

The question then arises as to why Jesus put adultery in the same category as murder. Leviticus 20:10 says, "The man who commits adultery with another man's wife, he who commits adultery with his neighbor's wife, the adulterer and the adulteress, shall surely be put to death." Murderers and adulterers deserve death, according to the law, and Jesus shows that the law is impossible to obey. What's going on?

A lot of this, I admit, is not comprehensible this side of heaven, but we had better find out why these two sins are considered equally reprehensible before we start building our lives on our own principles. Why was it so important that people not commit adultery? I submit that the reasons, whatever they are, are the same reasons we need to plant hedges around our hearts, eyes, hands, spouses, and marriages. If adultery is in the same class as murder, it is a threat not only to our marriages but also to our very lives.

Some have said that only a crazy person can commit murder. A man or woman has to lose contact with reality to become so angry or distraught or jealous that he or she can take another's life. I've found that adulterers suffer this same malady. They violate a vow they made years before, drag their wife and family through torture and disgrace, and set aside or reformat their entire set of values. How else could a man justify the chaos wrought by his actions?

A friend of mine once found himself pulled into a situation in which he was to officiate at a family meeting where an adulterous father tried to explain to his children, in front of his wife, why he was leaving her for another woman. One of this man's first assertions was that he had never really loved his wife. (To a person who believes that love is a feeling rather than an act of the will, falling out of love or deciding you never loved someone is a convenient rationalization.)

The teenage son said, "How, after all these years, can you say you don't love Mom? After all we've done together . . ."

The only way the man could live with himself was to tell himself lies, to reorder his standards. He said to his younger daughter, "Honey, tell me what you're thinking."

She looked up at him, fighting for composure. "I'm thinking I'm sad."

Adultery Causes Chaos

Adulterers are liars, and they are as good at it as alcoholics and addicts are.

Another friend of mine was awakened in the middle of the night by a call informing him of the infidelity of a good friend.

He couldn't believe it, so he went to see the man. "Dave," he said, "what's the story about you and this woman?"

Dave played dumb. "It's not true," he said, looking my friend squarely in the eye. "No way. Not me. Never have, never will."

"Wait a minute," my friend said. "What about all these allegations?" He proceeded with a litany of charges, names, dates, places.

"Someone's trying to frame me," Dave said. "Never happened."

What a relief! My friend wouldn't have to see this man confess to his wife, disappoint her, break her heart, ruin their marriage. It was good news . . .

. . . until two months later, when my friend's wife got a call from Dave's wife. She was hysterical. My friend and his wife raced to her home while Dave was away on business. She had discovered the affair and had a pile of evidence to prove it.

My friend was assigned to meet Dave at the airport upon his return. Rather than being met by his family as usual, Dave was puzzled to see my friend standing there solemnly. "It's over," my friend told him. "Your wife knows, and I know."

He led Dave to the parking lot, where Dave's car was jammed floor to ceiling with his belongings. There was barely room for the two men. Dave drove my friend home and then set out to look for a place to live. My friend watched him pull out of sight in the darkness, and he knew: Adultery causes chaos.

Adultery causes chaos.

An acquaintance once told me that, yes, he had been seeing another woman, but, no, he was not interested in her romantically and didn't think she was interested in him either. They were just friends. Middle of the night, sometimes all-night friends. He liked her baby daughter. Yeah, that was it. They had a lot in common, talked easily, liked each other's company. I told him that he didn't have the right to have a woman as a close friend when he was married and that it was slowly killing his wife.

He seemed to see the light and said he would break it off that night, and I returned to his wife with the wonderful news. That night, I watched from a distance as he met the woman after work. I saw them embrace and kiss before they left the state in her car. By the time he really came to his senses and pleaded for his wife to take him back—he terribly missed his four boys—the divorce was final. Adultery causes chaos.

Are You Guilty?

As much as television, movies, and videos try to convince us otherwise, adultery is not funny. The media have convinced too many people that adultery is no more serious than exceeding the speed limit.

"Everybody does it."

"This is a new age."

"Don't be so old-fashioned."

"Get with the program."

You can hardly watch a current sitcom without illicit sex as part of the story.

If the Bible deals with this modern issue, it had better do it in a sophisticated, up-to-date way or no one will pay any attention. What could a musty old religious tome have to say about life as we know it today?

Remember Leviticus 20:10? Adulterers are put to death.

Remember Matthew 5:27-28? Lust is adultery.

Are you guilty?

You may be guilty of more than lust. You may be guilty of adultery itself, and more than once. Be glad Jesus fulfilled the law for you, because even if your offense was the attitude and not the act, you are guilty.

But there is forgiveness. There is starting over. There is a future for you. John 8:3-11 tells this story:

Then the scribes and Pharisees brought to Him a woman caught in adultery. And when they had set her in the midst, they said to Him, "Teacher, this woman was caught in adultery, in the very act. Now Moses, in the law, commanded us that such should be stoned. But what do You say?" This they said, testing Him, that they might have something of which to accuse Him.

But Jesus stooped down and wrote on the ground with His finger, as though He did not hear. So when they continued asking Him, He raised Himself up and said to them, "He who is without sin among you, let him throw a stone at her first." And again He stooped down and wrote on the ground.

Then those who heard it, being convicted by their conscience, went out one by one, beginning with the oldest even to the last. And Jesus was left alone, and the woman standing in the midst. When Jesus had raised Himself up and saw no one but the woman, He said to her, "Woman, where are those accusers of yours? Has no one condemned you?"

She said, "No one, Lord."

And Jesus said to her, "Neither do I condemn you; go and sin no more."

Don't make the mistake of assuming Jesus was condoning adultery. He called her adultery sin and told her to "sin no more." I've always appreciated the irony in this story. Jesus said that the one "among you" without sin should cast the first stone. Have you ever thought about the fact that there *was* one among them who was without sin? It was Jesus Himself. And He chose not to cast a stone. His point was to label the accusers as adulterers, because indeed we all are—even if we have never committed the act. We may not have murdered, but we have hated; and we may not have committed adultery, but we have lusted. And Jesus says to us with the voice of loving forgiveness that rings through the ages, "Neither do I condemn you; go and sin no more."

Out of pure thanks and appreciation and wonder at that freeing compassion, we should want to obey.

But What about Temptation?

First Corinthians 10:13 says, "No temptation has overtaken you except such as is common to man; but God is faithful, who will not allow you to be tempted beyond what you are able, but with the temptation will also make the way of escape, that you may be able to bear it."

The problem with lust and its results is that it is difficult to resist and people try everything to win over it. They pray, they stand and fight, they resolve, when all the while our plan of attack is clear—and it's not a plan of attack at all. We are to retreat! As we've seen before, Paul wrote to his young friend in 2 Timothy 2:22, "Flee also youthful lusts; but pursue righteousness, faith, love, peace with those who call on the Lord out of a pure heart."

The problem with the temptation verse (1 Corinthians 10:13) is that people apply it too late. Ten minutes into foreplay with the wrong partner, they may be ready to seek that way of escape that was supposed to have come with the temptation. But that's just it: The escape comes with the temptation. It's preventive medicine, not first aid after you've already set your course on a path toward injury.

More Biblical Bases for Hedges

Need more evidence that there are biblical bases for planting hedges around your marriage? Psalm 89:40 implies that strongholds are brought to ruin when hedges are broken down. Job 1:10, cited earlier, implies that Job was so richly blessed—before God allowed him to be tested—because God had "made a hedge around him, around his household, and around all that he [had] on every side."

Jesus told a parable about landowners who planted vine-yards and protected them with hedges. When those hedges were trampled or removed, ruin came to those landowners (see Matthew 21:33-41).

We hold people and relationships much more precious than land or holdings. If we can keep from deceiving ourselves about our own resolve and inner strength, we will see the necessity for a healthy row of blossoming hedges that keep love in and infidelity out.

8

THE MAN IN THE MIRROR

Knowing our own weakness is one way to begin tilling the soil for the seeds that will grow the hedges to protect us.

Before I get into explaining my own hedges—which I listed in the introduction and which reveal my own weaknesses—I need to ask: What are yours?

A friend of mine has planted two hedges for his business life. First, he stays away from pornography, which has become more difficult this century than ever before, given the illusion of privacy via the internet and the pervasiveness of what is piped into almost every hotel room in the world.

Rather than pretend to be disgusted and turned off by it, he admits that porn can be seductive. It can be tantalizing. Although looking at pornography may result in revulsion with himself and wondering how he could ever be attracted to such a cheapening of God's gift of sexuality, he is more successful in fending it off by acknowledging in advance that it's something he's determined to avoid.

In hotels, he used to be able to tell the front desk to lock it out—something I used to do as well. Sometimes the clerk would act surprised or wonder aloud if he had children with him in spite of his reservation as a single. (I've told desk clerks, "Yes, there's a kid here. It's the big one talking to you right now.") My friend would clarify that he's alone and insist on the lock-out service. The problem now, though, is that most streaming services include a porn package that cannot be locked out. The best hedge against this temptation is to travel with a business partner so you can hold each other accountable.

I've had friends and even loved ones tell me that since they had gone many years without succumbing to the temptation of pornography, they believed they could surely travel on their own and not have to embarrass themselves by asking a desk clerk half their age to lock out the adult movies. But then a borderline sexy show on regular television whets their appetite for something racier, and with the seemingly innocuous touch of a button, they convince themselves that they're mature enough to satisfy their curiosity.

The key is preventive maintenance. Once that first step has been taken down the road of self-deceit and rationalization, there is no turning back. Each excuse sounds more plausible, and before he knows it, the typical male has satisfied every curiosity, every urge. Regardless of the remorse, the self-loathing, and the pledges, the pattern will repeat itself for as long as he refuses to flee. There is no other defense.

My friend's second hedge comes in the form of pictures he carries in his wallet of his wife and two daughters. These serve the usual function of reminding him of his loved ones and allowing him to brag about his beautiful family. But they also serve as a safety net, which he used several years ago when he found himself next to a beautiful, young, single woman on an airplane.

Normally he feigns fatigue and isn't interested in conversing during a long flight, but this woman was fun to look at and more fun to talk to. He asked her about herself. She sounded more interesting and exciting every minute. She was staying in the same city to which he was headed. She had a car and could give him a ride to his hotel. And why not? She seemed nice enough.

We're Not All the Same

To illustrate differences in styles and personalities, I must say that I would have hidden behind the hedge I planted years ago that does not allow me to accept a ride alone with an unrelated woman. I wouldn't trust my weak, self-deceiving, rationalizing mind once I was alone with a beautiful, willing female. My friend, however, used a different hedge and was able to accept the ride. When she asked about himself, he pulled out his wallet. Even before he showed her the photos of his wife and daughters, "It was as if they spoke to me right out of that wallet. They said, 'Thanks, Daddy, for being faithful to Mom and to us.'"

He smiled as he showed her the pictures and spoke lovingly of his family, especially of his wife, Jackie. The conversation mellowed and became friendly in a different sort of way from before. My friend rode with the woman to his hotel, shook her hand, and heard her say in farewell, "Say hi to Jackie for me."

"If you think I didn't want to spend the night with her," he says, "you're crazy."

But it wasn't worth his spiritual, mental, and family life. He used a hedge, one that wouldn't have worked for me, but one effective for him and his personality.

Some Things Are Black and White

In this age of rampant relativism, life simply does not seem as tidy as we may have once thought. Black-and-white issues tend to gray around the edges. But beware of assuming that nothing is absolute.

Some things are black and white.

You've heard the axioms *It takes two to tango* or *There are always two sides to an argument* or *There are exceptions to every rule.* Let me run down a few scenarios for you and see if you still buy into those "accepted truths."

I personally know of at least one divorce (the ultimate argument) where the wife was indeed an innocent and offended party. I'm not saying she was perfect or even someone I would want to be married to. I *am* saying that the offending party, the adulterer, the deserter, the abuser, in all his manic rages, never even accused his wife of anything remotely connected to justifiable biblical grounds for divorce.

Some things are black-and-white.

Again, hear me, I'm not saying—especially in this case—that the wife was a model spouse. She may not have even been a better-than-average wife. She was human. She made mistakes. She was impatient at times, shrewish and nagging at others, she admits. But not even her philandering husband would say she didn't love him in word and deed. He couldn't say she had ever broken her marriage promise. She had never done anything but try to keep a bad marriage together.

Now then, the black and white. The adulterer—the divorcer, the leaver—is the guilty party, the offending party, the one in the wrong. The stayer—the worker, the promise keeper, the admittedly imperfect one who never gave up, who never quit loving and trying, and who fought the sundering legal action—is innocent in this instance and offended.

I feel the need to make that clear because in the twenty-first century, it becomes easier to rationalize these things.

"They weren't right for each other from the beginning."

"Well, she was no prize."

"No wonder he went looking for love somewhere else."

And on and on.

Perhaps frustration was justified. Perhaps despair was justified.

Perhaps even a little self-pity and dreaming of how much better things might have been with someone else is understandable. But nothing justifies sexual sin. Nothing justifies breaking promises, living lies.

Admittedly, in many bad marriages there are two sides. Both are unfaithful. Both are mean and nasty and abusive, lying, promise breakers. Neither, however, may use the other's sins as justification for their own. And in those cases, yes, it takes two, there are two sides, and if we knew everything that went on behind closed doors, we wouldn't take sides.

Neither am I saying that it is always right for the offended party to stay. I believe that the God who is the author of life and the antithesis of death does not "call" an abused spouse to remain in a life- or health-threatening situation. While, yes, God hates divorce, and yes, a wife is to submit to her husband (and he to her, of course), no sane interpretation of Scripture requires a woman to stay with a man at the risk of life and health.

However, back to my point. Sometimes, things are black and white, and someone is guilty and someone is innocent. While it may usually—I repeat, *usually*—be wisest not to take sides, especially in the divorce of friends, there are times when you should learn all you can and cast your lot with the offended party.

That doesn't mean to be an enabler when a hurting person wants to spew venom about a former spouse. But it does mean assuring that friend that she is a person of value, that she was treated unfairly, that her trust was trampled, but that she still has loyal friends.

Some scriptural issues can be black and white but still difficult to explain. Because we are not God, we might have, for instance, written differently John 14:6: "Jesus said to him, 'I am the way, the truth, and the life. No one comes to the Father except through Me.'"

People much more theologically astute than I have written books on this statement, and, let's face it, it's exclusivist. As a layman, all I can tell you is that Jesus Himself said it, God ordained it, and John wrote it! It's in the Bible in black and white.

It's true.

It may not seem fair. We may not like arguing it or defending it, but those words sure set some parameters for our lives, don't they? If any devout, sincere, nice person can get to God in his own way, then the extent of our responsibility to mankind would be to encourage people to be nice. That's easier than telling a Buddhist, a Muslim, or a Jew that Jesus is the only way to God.

Amazingly, many devotees of the most prevalent religions are unaware of that statement by Jesus. Those who seem nicer and more tolerant than we are may say, "Our faith incorporates yours. We take the truth from all the prophets and holy men. We take the best from Confucius, Buddha, Muhammad, Jesus, and Moses, and we accept all."

What magnanimous people! What appealing religion! *We're all in this together*, they say. *Don't exclude those who choose a different path. Don't think you have a monopoly on truth. Let's share the truths and great teachings from all our faiths.*

One problem: Our Man doesn't fit. He's the One among all the others who says He's the only way. You can't have a harmonious quartet or quintet when one of the members is a self-proclaimed soloist.

When people of other faiths, or people with no faith who "really, really respect what Jesus was all about," find out that He said what He said, they often don't like Him anymore. They consider Him an egotist at best. But as Christian writer and theologian C. S. Lewis argued, to make the claim Jesus made, He had to be a liar, a lunatic—or Lord of all.

People who think the start and finish of Jesus' ministry came in the Sermon on the Mount need to be gently directed to His more radical statements. When people say, "I think Jesus was a great teacher and prophet, but I don't think he was God or the Son of God," they need to know that He Himself made those claims.

They can't have it both ways. Is a teacher great and wonderful even if he is deluded in thinking he is divine? I had many great teachers in my educational background, but if even my favorite would have said he was the only way to God, I'd have been out of there in a New York minute.

Jesus will not settle for being one of many. He's all there is, the only way to God, and there's no in-between on that. He's living proof of the smaller truth I'm espousing about this pedestrian subject of marriage and fidelity in the twenty-first century: Some things are black and white.

Custom-Make Your Hedges

Just as my friend used a different hedge from what I would have, likewise, there are temptations more difficult for some than for others. For instance, the temptation to frequent prostitutes happens to be one I can't identify with. I know it's a very real temptation and has been the ruin of Christians, even preachers, and that the book of Proverbs is replete with admonitions about and against it. It just happens, though, that this is an area in which I have never been tempted—although I was once propositioned.

I was on business in Cleveland and had booked a room at a well-known hotel chain, not realizing even on the ride in from the airport that this hotel sat in the seediest part of town. So I was stunned when I went out for a walk and found myself in the red-light district. While I might have been young and curious enough to be tempted to slip into an adult movie theater, my fear of a firebomb or a raid was sufficient defense. "Christian Writer among Dead in Adult Theater Fire" would have been a nice final page for my wife's scrapbook, eh? Fear of detection is not the most altruistic motive for avoiding such temptations, but use whatever works at the point of weakness.

It was dark, and the area seemed overrun with potential muggers. I was hurrying back to my hotel when a teenaged prostitute made me an offer I'm sure she thought I couldn't refuse. I was nearly paralyzed. I had always wondered what I would say. This girl was not unattractive, but I had not the slightest second thought of giving in to her suggestion. The question was what I would say.

I could have ignored her and kept walking, which I would do today. I could have looked shocked and disgusted and told her off, which would have been unkind. I could have witnessed to her. (I have friends who do that, but I don't recommend it unless you're with your wife or a group. Say the wrong thing while witnessing to an undercover cop and you'll find yourself, and your ministry, in the overnight lockup. Or, if you're alone, try explaining to someone who recognizes you just what you were saying to the woman on the corner.)

At the time, I was in my early twenties, and all my upbringing and training came to the fore. I was polite—maddeningly and, as I think about it, hilariously polite. I said, "No, thanks."

She looked disappointed. "Are you sure?"

"Yes, but thanks anyway."

"What you wanna be alone for tonight when you can be indulgin' yourself?"

"That's all right," I said. "I hope you won't be offended if I pass."

As she shrugged and trudged on, I thought, *"I hope you won't be offended"? What a stupid thing to say!* That girl was threatening my moral and spiritual health, trying to get me to jeopardize my marriage, encouraging me to go against everything I had ever been taught or believed, and I was polite! But someone who travels frequently or is tempted by such offers should consider custom-making a hedge against such situations.

Are You Lonesome Tonight?

I was with an older colleague in a topflight hotel in Detroit several years ago when we smelled perfume and heard a spraying sound near the door. He tiptoed over in stocking feet to discover that indeed someone was spraying perfume under the door. He swung it open to see a middle-aged woman in a miniskirt leaning seductively in the frame.

"You lonely, hon?" she asked.

"I'll never be that lonely," he said and shut the door. I wish I'd thought of that.

On the other hand, I heard a prominent preacher say that he once got on an elevator in a hotel in a big city and was greeted warmly by two beautiful young women. A glib, social type, he engaged them in friendly banter before they boldly asked him to join them in their room. "In the space of less than a minute, I had to make a decision," he says. "I was far from home. I could get away with this, in one sense." He knew it would be wrong, however, so he silently prayed for the strength to resist and left the elevator on his own floor.

It can be disappointing to hear that a man of God would have to talk himself out of something like that, but each man carries with him his own weaknesses and temptations. Whereas I have never been able even to imagine being attracted to or turned on by a woman who has had sex with others all day, I do plant hedges against being alone or working too closely with women I simply admire or like. That, to me, is more dangerous. I could see myself becoming attached to or enamored with someone I worked with if I didn't emphasize keeping everything on a professional basis. *Whatever your weaknesses, build your hedges against them.*

A Word of Caution

Just because I can't imagine ever being tempted by a prostitute doesn't mean I am cavalier or naïve about their areas and haunts. There are other forms of illegal activity that don't tempt me either, but I don't hang around their headquarters.

In other words, if you're tempted to cruise prostitution row, the way of escape is to do something else. Go somewhere else. While you have your wits about you—before you're at the edge of the abyss—set a rule for yourself that you won't drive within a certain number of blocks of the area for any reason. If you're tempted to cruise online, think filters and accountability.

Some hedges may appear ridiculous to you because they're unnecessary in your life—just like the one above is for me. I used to drive home right through an area where prostitutes frequented the corners. I knew enough not to look interested, which was easy because I truly wasn't. I was curious, sure, wondering about these sad girls with wasted bodies and faces, clearly addicted to drugs, waving at cars and trying to avoid detection by police. But tempting it was not.

A man I used to work with told me he drove through that same area, and as he was looking at one of the women while at a stoplight, she approached his car. She asked if he wanted a date. He said no, but she seemed friendly, so he asked her what the going rate was. She told him. He smiled at her, waved, and drove off.

I knew him. He would not have been any more attracted to a prostitute than I was, but he had been stupid. Somehow, even with the spate of documentaries and dramas about the world of prostitution, he had missed the fact that negotiating the price is the operative offense that can get you locked up. Had that woman been an undercover cop, he would have been arrested.

More Stupidity

Too many men are foolish in other ways. They think they can handle any temptation. Their resolve, their marriage, or their spirituality will carry the day. These men are self-deceived, and we all know too many of them.

No one wants to admit he has a problem or a weakness. I confess it bothered me when I heard the minister in the hotel elevator story above give that account. I wondered why he didn't admit to some other, less offensive temptation, like maybe the urge to spend more on a car than he should have. For some reason, we don't want our spiritual heroes to be human. Wives don't want their husbands to be human. Kids don't want their dads to be human. We'd all like to know someone who is so spiritual, so wise, and so disciplined that he would ignore or throw away a men's magazine left in his hotel room by the previous guest. I'll tell you, if I didn't throw it out upon first discovering it, ignoring it would be difficult.

> No one wants to admit he has a problem or a weakness.

No one likes to admit that. I can hear people saying, "How disgusting! Who would want to poison his mind with that trash?"

Certainly not I. Or would I? All I know to do, according to Paul's letter to Timothy, is to flee. Why? Because of what Paul also said in his letter to the Romans:

> For what I am doing, I do not understand. For what I
> will to do, that I do not practice; but what I hate, that
> I do. If, then, I do what I will not to do, I agree with the
> law that it is good. But now, it is no longer I who do it,
> but sin that dwells in me. For I know that in me (that is,
> in my flesh) nothing good dwells; for to will is present
> with me, but how to perform what is good I do not find.
> ROMANS 7:15-18

And in Romans 7:22-25 Paul told us:

> For I delight in the law of God according to the inward
> man. But I see another law in my members, warring
> against the law of my mind, and bringing me into
> captivity to the law of sin which is in my members.
> O wretched man that I am! Who will deliver me from

this body of death? I thank God—through Jesus Christ
our Lord!

So then, with the mind I myself serve the law of God,
but with the flesh the law of sin.

The only future in self-deceit is ruin. Let's quit kidding ourselves. No, we don't have to broadcast to the public every base
thought and urge, but in our heart of hearts, let's avoid denial. If
the greatest missionary in the history of Christendom could make
himself vulnerable by admitting that in his flesh dwelled no good
thing, who are we to think we should be above carnal drives and
desires?

My only regret since launching my hedges campaign years ago
is that occasionally some wonderful female colleague or new friend
will say, "I don't know how to act around you, whether I can touch
you or even shake your hand."

The last thing I want is a reputation as a guy desperately trying
to contain his lustful thoughts for everything in a skirt. As you'll
see later, I do trust myself to touch and embrace even women I'm
not related to. But I have strict guidelines and hedges because I
don't want to succumb to my own self-deceit.

Let's start planting some practical hedges.

PART TWO

BEGINNING THE PROCESS

Here are pragmatic ways to guard ourselves against our weaknesses. We can plant hedges only after we have determined where they need to grow.

9

THAT CONTROVERSIAL RULE

Hedge No. 1. Whenever I need to meet or dine or travel with an unrelated woman, I make it a trio. Should an unavoidable last-minute complication make this impossible, my wife hears it from me first.

This hedge—which, as I mentioned, has become known as the Billy Graham rule due to his strict observance of it—is about pure logic. Scripture is clear that Christians should "abstain from sexual immorality," for "this is the will of God" (1 Thessalonians 4:3).

So, you ask, *what is sexually immoral about meeting, dining, or traveling with an unrelated woman?* Nothing. But it also follows that if I'm not alone with a woman, I won't engage in immorality with her.

But you may still wonder, *What does one necessarily have to do with the other?* In other words, *If it's true that I won't commit adultery if I'm not alone with a woman, is it also true that if I'm alone with her, I will?* No, that's not logical. But logic does say that if I'm following the biblical injunction to abstain from even the "appearance of evil" (1 Thessalonians 5:22, KJV), I will also abstain from the evil itself.

My contention is that if you take care of how things *look*, you take care of how they *are*.

I once worked in a building that had a tiny window in every office door. When these were installed forty or fifty years prior, they were not intended to make immorality difficult. They were intended to eliminate suspicion and protect reputations. As long as that little eye to the outside world remained uncovered, no one felt free to attempt anything untoward, and just as importantly, no one else needed to suspect what went on behind closed doors. Were it not for those little windows, I would have felt obligated to invite my secretary to every brief meeting I had with a woman or to keep my door open.

Why? Am I really that weak or dangerous? Or are those with whom I might meet? No, I don't think so. But I don't want the reputations of the woman, my employer, my wife, or my Lord— not to mention myself—even questioned.

Risky Business

One of the saddest and scariest stories I've ever heard on this subject was about a young evangelist. He was just twenty-one, on fire for God, effective in his preaching and soul winning, and in great demand from local churches. He had preached several large crusades and was soon invited to an area-wide effort in a big church at which he would be the main speaker.

Though he was not yet even out of college, he was a protégé of international evangelist Sammy Tippit and was admired and considered wise. He didn't have a steady girlfriend, but he dated regularly at Bible college. Spiritually, he was alert and mature. He was, however, naïve.

The first night of the crusade, he supervised the counseling ministry in a large room near the pastor's study. A beautiful teenager I'll call Cindy asked if she could speak with him personally. He tried to assign her to someone else, but when she insisted that she needed to talk only with him, he agreed she could wait until he was finished with the others.

More than an hour after the crusade service had ended, the rest of the counselors and counselees had left, and he was alone with the young girl. A few minutes later, Cindy burst from the room, screaming, "He made a pass at me! He wanted to make love to me!"

That very night, the pastor of the host church and a small group of the crusade planners confronted the young preacher and demanded an explanation. He denied the girl's charge but had no witnesses. The girl had seemed an upstanding young woman in the church, and there was no reason for the pastor or staff to disbelieve her.

My contention is that if you take care of how things look, *you take care of how they* are.

"What did happen in that room?" the pastor demanded.

"To tell you that," the young man said, "would be to make an accusation behind someone's back. Which is what happened to me. I ask only that I be allowed to face my accuser."

The pastor canceled the rest of the crusade and agreed that the young woman should face the preacher in their presence. Two nights later, she showed up with her parents to a private board meeting. The pastor asked her to repeat her charges.

"She has already said all she has to say," her father said, her mother nodding and glaring at the accused.

The pastor said, "Would you, son, care to share your version of what happened?"

"No, sir," the evangelist said. "I see no future in that. Only she and I know the truth, and I cannot defend myself. I'd just like to say this to her. Cindy, you know what happened and what didn't happen in that room. If you don't tell the truth, I will be branded and may never preach again. This will damage my reputation and that of this church and even that of God. If I did what you say I did, I deserve no better, but we both know that is not the truth. I'm begging you in the name of Christ to set the record straight."

The silence hung heavy as the board and her parents watched her face contort until the tears began to flow. "I lied," she said quietly. "I'm sorry. I lied. He didn't make a pass at me; I made a pass at him. When he turned me down, I was so embarrassed and ashamed and angry that I made up that story. I'm so sorry!"

Had that young evangelist not had the wisdom to face his accuser in just that manner, his ministry might have been ruined forever. And had not God worked in that young girl's heart, she might have sat there silently, refusing to change her story.

That preacher is no longer young. He has never again allowed himself to be alone in a room with a female to whom he is not related. Along with his spiritual wisdom came a painful, almost fatal farewell to naïveté. He might have been embarrassed that night, early in his ministry, if he'd had to ask someone to stay with him while he counseled the young woman, or if he'd had to tell her that he could see her only in the sanctuary. But now he sees embarrassment, or sometimes even the risk of offending, as a small price for protecting all those reputations.

A Movable Feast

Notice that I include dining alone with my meeting and traveling prohibitions. I don't know why, but there is something particularly personal and even somewhat intimate about eating with someone. If that weren't true, why do so many dates revolve around food?

My embargo against dining alone with an unrelated woman is also for my wife's sake. Dianna is not the jealous type, but this way I don't have to keep track of every lunch partner and make sure I tell her about each one before someone else does. People love to say, "Oh, I saw your husband having lunch with so-and-so the other day," with that lilt in their voice that begs to know if anything is going on.

My intention is that if someone were to tell Dianna I had been seen with someone alone, she would immediately say, "No, he wasn't," because she knows that if that were to happen, she would have known about it first.

Once my secretary and I invited a friend of hers to have lunch with us. At the last minute, the friend was unable to go. We just changed our plans, had the lunch delivered, and enjoyed it in the office with the door open. I mentioned the situation to my wife in advance, as a courtesy.

I fully understand how legalistic this hedge may appear—and I can't deny I've been criticized for it, once even berated by a friend's wife who felt insulted that I would not dine with her alone. I tried to assure her I meant no offense and was thinking of her reputation as much as my own, but I'm not sure I convinced her.

> Over the years, as we saw marriage after marriage fail and family after family suffer, my prudish-appearing rules made more sense.

The first few times my secretary and I changed our plans because a third party was unavailable, even she may have thought I was being ridiculous. She had no designs on me, and vice versa, though we were friends. I'm sure I seemed to be straining at a gnat. But over the years, as we saw marriage after marriage fail and family after family suffer, my prudish-appearing rules made more sense.

There will always be times, of course, when rules cannot be followed to the letter. During my years as a publishing executive in Chicago, I occasionally found it necessary to drop a woman colleague off at one office building or another. Before the advent of ubiquitous cell phones, sometimes this came up when it was inconvenient or impossible to let my wife know in advance. It would have been silly to wait until I could either tell her or ask permission. I told her later, and though she never demanded it, she always appreciated my candor. On those rare occasions when I did question the reputation of one with whom I might have to meet or dine or travel alone, I didn't think twice. I didn't call to inform Dianna or to ask her permission. I just didn't go.

On the Road

Travel is chock-full of dangerous possibilities for appearances and behavior. Even if every motive is pure, how does it look for a man and a woman who aren't married to each other to be on a long trip together—in a car, on a plane, in a cab, at the same hotel, even if in separate rooms?

I once had to travel to a distant city with a female manager who reported to me, so I asked her to select someone to go with us. The young woman she chose woke up ill on departure day, and I didn't learn about it until I arrived at the airport. The manager was also a friend of our family, which helped, and though she was single and close to my age, our relationship was such that we didn't worry about anything happening. We worried most about how the trip would look.

Because originally she had planned to room with the younger woman, we had thought nothing of booking our seats together on the plane and sharing a ride to—and staying at—the same hotel. All those arrangements had been made, but I was willing to absorb the cost of canceling them if necessary.

My first query was to the manager herself. She expressed her knowledge of, trust in, and respect for me. She said she had no problem traveling with me, but that she would understand if I chose not to go.

With a phone call from the airport, I passed the buck to my wife. She laughed. The fact that I had called her and had made a practice of keeping her informed of such seeming improprieties for years gave Dianna the confidence to immediately agree to the trip.

Advice from One Who Knows

Sadly, many pastors and other Christian leaders fall into sexual temptation because of a common problem. They have planted no hedges, and suddenly they find themselves counseling weeping, exasperated women who seem to have a lot to offer but are frustrated in bad marriages. They wish their husbands were more spiritual, were more popular, had more leadership qualities, were more authoritative, more patient, better listeners, men of the Word, men of prayer.

And guess what? The pastor or leader fills the bill on every point. The woman may be surprised to find herself falling for him, but once she has, she'll find the fact difficult to hide. And the pastor may at first innocently enjoy being so revered by a woman who needs him. If his wife is nagging him for spending too much time at church or in his ministry, he may begin looking forward to private counseling sessions with a woman who worships him, eats out of his hand, and gives him her full attention.

Male pastors and other Christian leaders need hedges as much as, if not more than, the rest of us. If they counsel women at all—and they would, in most cases, do better to assign them to some wise, older women in the church—they should counsel with the door open and an administrative assistant close by. Meetings with any female staff member or parishioner should take place only in public or with at least one other person there.

Billy Graham established this rule for himself early in his career as a personal code of conduct, in essence a self-imposed practice meant to avoid the appearance of impropriety or any situation that could potentially compromise his biblical moral and ethical standards.

The rule became well known and has been followed by many men in various professions, especially those in leadership roles, to set boundaries and protect against any potential dilemmas. Ironically, however, it has also been criticized for being restrictive and perpetuating gender bias. Even vigorous defenders of the #MeToo movement—whom I naïvely assumed would applaud such an approach—often refer to this rule as offensive and demeaning to women.

Former US Vice President Mike Pence was widely vilified for adhering to the Billy Graham rule, often based on concerns about gender discrimination or potential limitations it might impose on women in the federal government. Critics argue that the rule perpetuates the notion that men and women cannot have professional relationships without risking inappropriate behavior. This view suggests that my rule assumes that men lack self-control and implies that women are a constant temptation or potential threat. Critics also argue that such a rule can hinder a woman's career advancement opportunities.

As you might imagine, I disagree and maintain that women should establish the same hedge. To my mind, a female CEO or leader of any kind would demonstrate strength and conviction if she followed the rule and avoided even the appearance of impropriety.

But again, I prefer to speak only for men, believing that my dining and traveling hedges should never be trampled when it comes to our spending time with unrelated women. And the only reason the standards for leaders are stricter than for us rank-and-file types is that, in most cases, more is at stake.

For all of us, however, the price of suspicion is high, and the price of infidelity is even higher. There are more hedges to plant.

10

TACTILE DANGER

Hedge No. 2. I am careful about touching. Although I might shake hands or squeeze an arm or shoulder in greeting, I embrace only dear friends or relatives, and only in front of others.

Touchy, Touchy!

Again, I realize how uptight this hedge can make me appear. Maybe being so touchy about touching seems foreign to you and you don't need to plant this hedge. So be it. As I've said, you may need hedges in areas where I don't. But be careful not to simply thumb your nose at this one until you hear me out.

I don't know when touching returned to vogue in the United States, but I recall clearly when the encounter-group, get-in-touch-with-yourself philosophy finally reached the church. I was in high school in the midsixties, and somewhere around that time, something new began.

Worship became more expressive. People became more emotional. And maybe because there was a significant Jesus People movement heading east from California, and that movement had originated among street people and hippies accustomed to more openness than the rest of society, certain things became more acceptable in the church.

Of course, this wasn't all bad. I was visiting a camp when I was about fifteen, and after a particularly moving evening of testimonies, singing, and speaking, people were weeping and swaying as they sang with arms around each other's shoulders. Believe it or not, that was interesting and different—at least in the evangelical circles I ran in at that time in the Midwest.

What impressed me after that camp service was the freedom everyone felt to hug each other. I had a girlfriend I didn't mind hugging, but I wasn't crazy about anyone else hugging her. I was shocked to see high school girls hugging camp leaders I knew were married, but it didn't seem to bother anyone else.

That was at a time of life when I would have enjoyed hugging any female, but still, it didn't seem right. How old that makes me feel now, and how (sorry) out of touch. At that age, you wonder if you can control yourself if given the opportunity to embrace a beautiful girl. Suddenly it seemed okay to hug anybody who was as happy as you were, because we were brothers and sisters in Christ.

I was slow to catch on to the joy of this new freedom in Christian circles, and it was hard to keep emotions and feelings in check when you could embrace an adult woman, plus all the girls your own age. It seemed to have happened all of a sudden, and there was something spiritual about it.

The rub (pardon the pun) was that—unless I was the only pervert around—I had a good idea that most of the guys my age were less spiritual and more sensual and physical about all this, regardless of our high ideals. And we did have high ideals. As I mentioned, one of my deepest desires was to remain sexually pure—a virgin until marriage. This I did, with God's (and a chaste girlfriend's) help, but, I confess, this new wrinkle in social behavior was of little assistance.

Say I was a hot-blooded teenager if you want, but this new openness to embracing was both a dream come true and a nightmare for the two sides of my nature. Christian psychologist Dr. James Dobson says that outside of hunger, the most powerful of all the human urges is the sexual appetite.[1] He adds that Christians have the same biochemical forces within their bodies that non-Christians do, and I can add from experience that teenagers, especially males, are bursting with erotic yearnings.

I know we're talking about decades ago, so to you it may seem like the Dark Ages. But how far we've come as a society and as a church since then is staggering. We might not want to admit that maybe things were better (even in the church) before the sexual revolution, but we have to ask ourselves: Were infidelity, divorce, and scandal as rampant then?

No, I'm not blaming these problems on a new openness to touching and hugging, but I know of people who fell in love because they enjoyed and looked forward to what began as a spiritual expression of brotherly and sisterly love.

> Suddenly it seemed okay to hug anybody who was as happy as you were, because we were brothers and sisters in Christ.

I saw this totally from my own narrow, adolescent viewpoint back then. I naïvely told myself that women weren't as interested in sex as men were and that adults certainly weren't as sexually on fire as teens. I was way too young to know the sexual responses of males and females.

I could be turned on by the very thought of something sensual. Seeing was even better. Touching, embracing—well, that was just short of making love, wasn't it? How could I have known then that embracing a woman might be almost the culmination of lust on my part, while it might be just the beginning of arousal for her? Am I saying that this new freedom to express ourselves to each other is wrong, sinful, dirty, or inappropriate? No.

I admit that the church needed thawing, some warming to each other. In the twenty-first century, men and women particularly needed to loosen up around each other, talk more, get to know each other better, and, yes, maybe even touch each other once in a while.

But back in the day, beyond the healthy exception of certain ethnic groups, men did not touch each other either—except for a formal or macho handshake, back slap, or thump on the rump during a ball game. I can't speak to the effect this new unpretentiousness might have had on men with a bent toward homosexuality, but one such friend of mine admitted it brought terrible temptation.

As I've grown older, I can acknowledge more of the good that came from the new style. I'm much more comfortable around women, and because it's now appropriate to greet them with a squeeze on the arm or even a warm but proper embrace, I feel better about my relationships. There can be a certain friendly and even spiritual intimacy that doesn't cross the line to impropriety or sensuality. My understanding and comfort level with this is due in part to my own maturity (praise the Lord, the heavy testosterone season of youth is pretty much past), but it's also because of the hedge I'm discussing here.

If I embrace only dear friends or relatives and only in the presence of others, I am not tempted to make the embrace longer or more impassioned than is appropriate. I like hugging women. It can be friendly. But if I allowed myself to embrace just anyone, even dear friends, in private, I would be less confident of my motives.

For instance, what would happen if I just lingered an instant to see what kind of reaction I might get? And let's say that the reaction was encouraging. We might both pretend it didn't happen, but what about next time? Would we not be carefully checking each other out to see if what we thought we felt the first time was accurate? And what if it was? At what point would we overtly embrace passionately, silently declaring our feelings for each other?

I don't know, and I don't want to know. That's why I keep such activity public, ensuring its appropriateness.

A Funny Memory

I have a cousin a few years younger. She's married and has kids. We've been long-distance buddies for years. Once I was in her state at a writers' conference, and she and her husband invited me for dinner. I waited for her while chatting with a woman from the conference, having idly mentioned that my cousin was coming to pick me up.

Oddly, we happened to be discussing this very subject of planting hedges around marriages. The woman had read my magazine article on the subject and was telling me some of the hedges she and her husband had planted.

A car slowly pulled up, and I recognized my cousin behind the wheel. I said my goodbyes, but as I hurried out, my cousin left the car and headed toward me. Youthful, tanned, and in shorts, she was striking and attractive. "Your cousin, huh?" the woman said, laughing. "I'll bet!"

My cousin had a child sleeping in a car seat in the back, and I was tempted to drag him out and display him to prove we had a chaperone. My cousin was normally a person I would embrace after not having seen her for a long time, but I decided against it for the sake of appearances. She got a good laugh out of the incident.

A Not-So-Funny Memory

Early in my journalism career, a young copy boy on the midnight shift of our paper endured a trauma with his brother, a wild kind of a guy. The brother lived in Oregon, and though he'd had drug and alcohol problems in the past, he had somehow landed a job as a security guard. One night after work, while at a party, he scuffled with someone, drew his gun, and shot the man, killing him.

My friend, as you can imagine, was distraught. He worried

constantly about his brother. Would he be sentenced? Would he commit suicide? Would he get the death penalty? My friend could hardly work. He was a good friend of our managing editor, a man twenty years his senior. The editor and his wife had taken a liking to the young man and encouraged him in his career. Both had been sympathetic to his worries over his brother and even helped him financially so he could travel to visit him.

Upon returning from that visit, my friend was convinced that his brother was in worse shape emotionally and psychologically than ever. Rather than help calm his fears, the trip had only upset my friend more. He visited the managing editor's home one night, looking for consolation and advice. The editor was gone. The editor's wife embraced my friend and rocked him as he wept for almost half an hour.

What started as an innocent, sympathetic embrace, an act of compassion, turned to passion.

This went on for two more nights before my friend came back with the shocking story that this woman, almost a mother figure to him, had made what he considered a pass at him. We scoffed, assuming he was bragging at best, lying at worst. The next night, he said he had made out with her for twenty minutes.

She was a woman with a husband who had other priorities. She was a woman who, upon marrying (as Helen Rowland was quoted in *Reader's Digest* years ago), "exchange[d] the attention of all other men she knew for the inattention of one."[2] She was starved for passion, and she found it where she could.

My friend was not without fault, but he was weak and vulnerable. Once she had taken advantage of him, there was no turning back. A marriage ended, and an affair began. There was no future in it for either of them, but they still played it out.

What started as an innocent, sympathetic embrace, an act of compassion, turned to passion.

Different Strokes

This entire subject of hugging and touching may not present a problem for you as it does for others. If you have never been turned on by the embrace of a friend, you may think this ridiculous. For you, perhaps it is. But if a person you embrace or who embraces you has a problem, beware.

There are times, places, and situations where physical touch is the only appropriate response. It's therapeutic, loving, and kind. There are other instances in which the same response is overkill.

A dear friend of ours recently suffered a terrible tragedy, losing the two people closest to her in the world in an accident in which she also was severely injured. This friend is close enough that I felt free to embrace her in public regularly. Now that she was in the deepest physical and emotional agony a person could endure, I didn't think twice about holding her hand as we talked or even resting my hand on her head as I would with a child in pain. My wife was also there, and this seemed the most logical and normal behavior.

In another context, at another time, a different set of actions would be appropriate. I love this woman in the purest nonromantic sense. I felt deeply for her and wanted her to know it. In another situation or circumstance, I would want to guard appearances by responding differently.

The matter of touching and being touched, embracing and being embraced, is as much a matter of common sense and decency as it is of ethnic background and custom. Because of the conservative way I was raised, I tread carefully in this area. If it doesn't happen to be an issue with you, I recommend only that you be sensitive to the attitudes and interpretations of those you choose to touch.

11

WATCH YOUR MOUTH

Hedge No. 3. If I pay a woman a compliment, it is on clothes or hairstyle, not on the person herself. Commenting on a pretty outfit is much different, in my opinion, from telling a woman that she herself looks pretty.

Okay, another seemingly confining hedge that might hit you as overwrought. But am I dealing here only with semantics? I think not. I still remember the first time, in the eighth grade, I mustered the courage to tell a girl "You look nice today." I was so nervous, and gushing that compliment was so disabling that it didn't even cross my mind to study her reaction.

She thanked me, but clearly I had made her feel uncomfortable too. Was she as affected as I was? I mean, I was so afraid of girls at that point that even adding, "How are ya?" at the end of a greeting was too much to consider.

Girls might call me by name and say hi. I would say, "Hi." They would add, "How are ya?" I'd say, "Fine," and keep moving. Why didn't I add, "How are you?"

Conversation, my mother tried to teach me, was like a tennis match. "Someone lobs one to you; you lob it back."

But I was in high school before I marshaled the courage to do that. The results were amazing. A girl I thought was gorgeous greeted me and asked how I was. I said, "Fine" and asked how she was. She assured me she was great and that she was glad I was fine. And she smiled at me. That alone was enough of a payoff. I had a limited enough self-image to know there was no future in a relationship with her. After all, I hardly knew her. But having a normal and polite, albeit empty, conversation with her provided its own euphoria.

So you can see what an accomplishment it had been in junior high for me to have summoned the fortitude to actually tell a girl she looked nice. I lived on that high for days, only to realize after a week or so that the girl was carefully avoiding me. Had I upset her? Scared her? Made her think I was interested in her?

Nothing was worse at that age than having someone you were not interested in pursue you. I certainly didn't want to be that guy. I wasn't cool or "in," wasn't a great dresser, and didn't have money. I was invisible. The only girls I attracted were those who knew they couldn't land someone impressive. When they chased me, I ran. And now I knew how they felt.

I even sent that girl a Valentine's Day card, one my brother had dreamed up. It included several small slips of paper with various flowers drawn on them. The card itself was a poem, instructing the recipient to send back to me one of the flowers. For instance, "If I am the one you chose, send me back the big, red rose." There were flowers that would tell me to be patient, to wait, or to keep trying, and there was even a dandelion with the verse, "If I waste my time in tryin', send me back the dandelion."

I waited and waited. I was ignored and even avoided at school by her until it got to the point where I would have been happy even to get the dandelion back. I merely wanted to know if she was aware of my existence. Maybe she had never received the card. The worst possible reaction was no reaction. Valerie, if you're out there, I need to tell you that I'm happily married and it's too late. If the rose merely got lost in the mail and you thought I had ignored you after that, what can I say? I'm sorry. (She sure looked nice that day. I just wish I could remember her last name.)

Lessons

In retrospect, I realize what I did wrong. Had Valerie been pining away for me, my compliment on how nice she looked might have thrilled her. But since my approach clearly came as a surprise, I should have emphasized her clothes and not the person. I should have been just slightly less personal, which is what I know to do now when complimenting any woman other than my wife. I don't have the right to tell a woman how she herself looks, though it might be appropriate to comment on her clothes or hair.

I base part of this hedge on my own reaction to how men talk to my wife. Dianna is tall, dark, and stunning—a head turner. It makes me proud to see men do a double take when they see her. If they keep staring, though, I stare right back until they notice that she's with me.

Dianna is typical of striking women unaware of their beauty and its impact. If I thought she were looking for compliments, it might bother me, but I'm used to the fact that she gets many. And I know she is truly beautiful as opposed to merely sexy, because she gets just as many compliments from women as from men. (In my experience, straight women compliment each other only on their beauty, not on their seductiveness.)

For some reason, it doesn't bother me if a man comments on my wife's hair or makeup or clothes. But if he should say that she looks pretty or is gorgeous or beautiful, that's too personal. Interestingly, either kind of compliment makes her uncomfortable, but she agrees that the personal approach is worse.

As a hedge, I stop short of the purely personal compliment, both because it's too intimate and because you can never be sure of the reaction. Some women would be offended at such familiarity, and men who talk to women that way tend to get reputations for it.

I know a man who is known not only for talking to and about women that way but also for hanging around them whenever he gets the chance. He always chats with the best-looking women at work, at church, or at a party. At conventions, he spends most of his time at the swimming pool talking to the prettiest women.

I stop short of the purely personal compliment, both because it's too intimate and because you can never be sure of the reaction.

I don't know him well enough to know whether his marriage is strong, but you can imagine what people will think if a rumor of infidelity ever makes the rounds. Innocent or not, he won't have a chance to survive it.

I rarely get complimented about my looks, but occasionally I'll wear something people like, and they say so. If a woman tells me she likes my tie, jacket, or hat, I don't assume she's on the prowl or frustrated by a bad marriage. I merely feel complimented.

Hearing Voices

On the uncommon occasion when a woman compliments the way I look, I confess I'm uncomfortable. Like anyone else, I have certain needs, and among those are what Dr. James Dobson calls emotional requirements: love, acceptance, belonging, caring, and tenderness.[1] My goal is to seek the fulfillment of those needs within the context of my own marriage.

Dr. Dobson says that there are certain voices that can lure you from a life of giving yourself to your spouse and children, working, paying the bills—toward infidelity. These are pleasure ("Come on, have fun; life is passing you by!"), romanticism (someone who cares, someone who is interested in you as a person, someone who wants to love you), sex (the pure pleasure of the physical act), and ego needs (someone finding you attractive for your mind, taste, or talent).

Dr. Dobson ranks sex at the low end of the scale of these reasons and puts ego needs at the top for both men and women. For women, he says, romanticism may be a close second, depending on the health of the marriage, and sex may be more important to men than to women because of the differences in biological makeup.[2]

The late James L. Johnson, on the flyleaf of his book *What Every Woman Should Know About a Man*, called sex "the strange and mysterious drive of the God-given chemistry that has shaped nations, destroyed kingdoms, and brought ruin or ecstasy to millions from the beginning of time."[3]

The problem with these voices that would lure us from normal life is that they're lying voices. They promise something other than simply another normal life. But if we run off with another woman—even if we do find more pleasure, more romance, more sex, and more of our ego needs fulfilled—a normal life still has to be dealt with. In fact, the new relationship may prove more burdensome than the one we left because of alimony and childcare expenses from the previous marriage.

As Dr. Dobson says, "the grass may be greener on the other side of the fence, but it still has to be mowed."[4]

Go Ahead, Make Her Day

The problem with ego needs and the need for romance, especially in a woman's life, is that they are hidden, unseen factors that men need to take into consideration when talking to women. We may innocently think it'll make a woman's day if we pay her a compliment that borders on the personal. So, rather than telling her that her sweater is beautiful and asking if she made it (implying that if she made it, she's incredible, and if she bought it, she has great taste), we tell her *she* looks great in it.

How do we know if perhaps the pleasure and romance, and

even the sex and ego strokes, haven't long since evaporated from her marriage? How do we know that she hasn't been longing for just this sort of attention from her husband? How do we know she hasn't given up on ever getting any more positive strokes from him, and that this personal approach from us may reach deep needs of which even she is hardly aware?

I want to be careful not to make women in bad marriages sound so weak and dependent that they live and die for any personal interest on the part of other men. But in individual cases, we don't know, do we? It never ceases to amaze me when I hear about another wife who has been abused or cheated on.

> Planting a hedge that allows you to compliment only a woman's taste in styles and clothes frees you to be friendly, outgoing, and encouraging to women without being suspected of anything worse.

Several years ago, a visiting preacher friend counseled the middle-aged wife of a pillar in our church. Her husband, a leading evangelical, had been in the ministry for more than forty years.

She confided in the evangelist that she had been a psychological prisoner in her own home for decades and had been physically abused during her entire marriage. She was nearly suicidal but said that something in the evangelist's sermon had given her a glimmer of hope. My friend told her there was nothing he could do for her until she was prepared to tell someone in authority—her pastor, her husband's superiors, or the police—about her husband. She was unwilling to do that.

Her husband is dead now, and my friend lost track of her. Sadly, however, her daughter must have suffered all those years too. A few years after marrying seemingly happily and starting a family—and several years before her father died—she disappeared for a few days and committed suicide a hundred miles from home.

I tell that sordid story to make the point that we never know what kinds of wounds and pains a person carries to church every

Sunday. The woman in the account above would probably not have been vulnerable to an approach by any man except for an extremely kind, gentle, godly person. But what about the others? What about those we know just as little about?

No doubt a case could be made for the fact that some women wouldn't detect the difference between a compliment of their hair or dress versus of themselves as persons. However, there is a difference, even if it registers only subliminally. Planting a hedge that allows you to compliment only a woman's taste in styles and clothes frees you to be friendly, outgoing, and encouraging to women without being suspected of anything worse.

Best Friends

Years ago, I had a boss who told me a story that illustrates the dangers I've been discussing here. A friend of his, Noah, was suspected of taking too much interest in a female teacher at the school where he coached. Noah insisted that there was nothing going on, but as rumor after rumor persisted, my boss felt obligated to confront him.

"If there's nothing going on between you and Isabella," my boss said, "why don't you quit spending so much time with her?"

"I like her," Noah said. "And she likes me. Is there anything wrong with having a friend of the opposite sex?"

"It depends on how your wife feels about it," my boss said.

"My wife hates it, but she's never been a friend to me."

My boss counseled him to break off the relationship. Within six months, Noah and Isabella divorced their spouses and married each other. Noah finally confessed to my boss that they had been intimate almost from the beginning, "It all started with my telling her how pretty she looked every day," he said. "She said she had been starved for that kind of attention, because she worked so hard at looking good and no one—she emphasized *no one*—ever seemed to notice."

"Except you," my boss said.

"Except me," Noah said, smiling. He was thrilled. He had found the girl of his dreams. No matter that two marriages and five children had been caught in the typhoon.

And neither Noah nor Isabella pledged that they would be truer to each other than they'd been to their first spouses, either. Noah never said he would quit complimenting women personally, and Isabella never said she would quit looking for the same from men other than her husband. For Noah to have kept the second marriage intact, he would have had to realize he was competing with anyone who thought his wife looked good and had the guts to tell her.

Apparently, he couldn't keep up with the competition. The marriage lasted fewer than four years, and it was Isabella who left him for an older man. (How long would you give that relationship?)

Something about being dumped brought Noah to his senses. He realized what he had done to his wife, and he pleaded with her to take him back. Even though she felt that as a divorced woman she was not free to marry anyone else, she didn't trust him. She was still in such pain that she asked for time to think it over.

He couldn't wait, and he married again. Chaos.

There Is a Way

Sometimes it feels great to compliment a woman other than your wife in a personal way, and you sense that it would be a good thing to do. In cases like that, I talk it over with Dianna first. We had a friend who was dumped by her husband. He tried to justify taking up with another married woman by telling anyone who would listen that despite her image, his wife was a shrew—cold, mean, unattractive, and dull.

Maybe behind closed doors she was all that, but my wife and I felt we knew her well enough and had seen her in enough situations to know that she was sweet, spiritual, a good mother, and a loyal and loving wife. She may not have been the hottest thing in town or the most fashionable, but she had certainly done nothing to justify her husband's adultery.

After planning, almost scripting, our approach, Dianna and I made sure we ran into her after church one Sunday night. With my arm around my own wife but looking directly into that suffering woman's eyes, I said, "You're not going to let what Ethan says convince you that you're not pretty or attractive or exciting, are you?"

She blushed and shook her head. I would not have felt free to say that without my wife at my side. Dianna added, "We know how much you have to offer, and if Ethan can't see that, he's just wrong. If he follows through with this, it'll be his loss, not yours."

As a rule, we make it a point not to take sides in separations and divorces, but when there is obvious adultery, we feel little loyalty to the offending party, friend or not.

To quote James Dobson once more: "Marriage is an institution designed to meet individual needs. The key is for husband and wife to meet each other's needs and for other people to mind their own business."[5]

12

BE CAREFUL
WHAT YOU ASK FOR

Hedge No. 4. I avoid flirtation or suggestive conversation, even in jest.

My late father, a police chief, firearms expert, and marksman, once told me that prayer is like looking down the barrel of a loaded gun. "You're likely to get what you're asking for."

I put flirtation and suggestive conversation in the same category as a loaded gun. Maybe that's because I believe in the power of words, written and spoken. Have you ever noticed that compliments and flattery are always heard? People have reminded me of compliments I've given years before and almost forgotten. They remember criticism, too, but flattery all the more.

> I put flirtation and suggestive conversation in the same category as a loaded gun.

Idle flirting can get people in trouble because often the other person needs and badly wants attention. Not many years ago, I slipped from behind this hedge, not intending to flirt but rather to be funny. It didn't get me into serious trouble, but I was certainly reminded of the reason for my hedge.

On a business trip, a woman colleague and I were going to go out to dinner with a male associate. When she came to pick me up, she was dressed and made up in flashy, coordinated colors that demanded comment. I should have just said something about her clothes, but instead—since she's always a good audience for my humor—I said the first funny thing that popped into my mind: "My, don't you look delicious."

She laughed, and I hoped she knew I meant that her colors reminded me of fruit, and not that I wished to devour her.

As soon as our third party arrived, she told him what I had said. He gave me a look that would have put a wart on a gravestone, but what could I say? I couldn't deny it, and it was too late to explain.

Men, of course, are just as susceptible to flattery as women. Most people think that the man in Proverbs heading down the road of destruction to the harlot's bed had followed his lust for sex. Surely that was part of it, but the text indicates that he was also seduced by her words. Proverbs 7:4-5 says, "Say to wisdom, 'You are my sister,' and call understanding your nearest kin, that they may keep you from the immoral woman, from the seductress who flatters with her words." And Proverbs 7:10, 21 says, "There a woman met him, with the attire of a harlot, and a crafty heart. . . . With her enticing speech she caused him to yield, with her flattering lips she seduced him."

Keep Humor in Its Place

It's widely known that funny people speak the truth through humor. They may exaggerate how upset they are that someone is late by looking at their watch and saying, "Oh, glad you could make it!" But beneath that joke is a barb of truth. The jokester has slipped in a little lecture without having had to embarrass anyone by saying, "Hey, pal, we agreed on six o'clock, and now here you come at six thirty! What's the deal? Get your act together!"

But the same thing happens when someone tries to be funny in a flirtatious manner. A man tells a woman, "Why don't we run off together? Tell that good-for-nothing husband of yours you got a better offer, eh?"

How's a woman supposed to react to that? The first time, she may think it's funny because it's so far out of the realm of possibility. Each successive time Mr. Comedian says something like that, it gets more irritating. That is, unless the woman has always been attracted to him and has problems at home. Then she might hope there's truth behind the humor.

Often there is. The only time a funny flirter is totally putting someone on is when he throws his arm around a particularly old or unattractive woman and tries to give her a thrill by saying something she's probably never heard before. "Hey, gorgeous! Where have you been all my life?"

Women like that know better than to believe such drivel, but they may long to hear it anyway. A colleague of mine once toyed with just such a woman by caressing her cheek. "I'm melting," she said, and I sensed she meant it.

The real danger comes when the man is pretending to be teasing but would really love to flirt. A woman may not suspect the truth behind his humor, and if she responds in kind, there's the opportunity for misunderstanding. Or worse, she may indeed suspect that he means it, and then there's the opportunity for real understanding.

> The real danger comes when the man is pretending to be teasing but would really love to flirt.

Such a tragedy occurred at a church in Michigan where a couple flirted humorously for almost ten years. They did this in front of everybody, including their spouses, who laughed right along with them. The flirters were never seen alone together, because they never *were* alone together.

Then came the day when the woman's husband was sick and in the hospital. She needed rides back and forth, and her friend and his wife provided them. No one suspected anything, but on one of those rare occasions when it was just the man doing the driving, the wife of the sick man told him how difficult and cold her husband had been for years.

The flirters began to see each other on the sly until the day came when she told him she had always hoped he'd meant what he said when he had teased her about how wonderful she was, how good she looked, and how he wished he'd met her before she was married. Whether he'd really meant it was irrelevant now that she had declared herself. The fact was, he admitted later, that this was what he had wanted all along. He would never have made the first move, however. He had cloaked his true desires behind humor. A little crisis, a little honesty, and suddenly years of innocent flirting blossomed into an affair.

Innocent Humor

I worked at a camp one summer during high school. One week, one of the female counselors, about a year older than me, happened to share my last name. We were not related and had never seen each other before, and when we were introduced, we didn't make much of the coincidence. While Jenkins is not as common as Smith or Jones, neither is it as unique as Higginbotham or Szczepanik.

One night after the campers were in bed, a bunch of us staffers, Miss Jenkins included, were watching a football game on television. A couple of the guys started kidding her and me about being married. We were both so young, naïve, and insecure that we just blushed.

For some reason, I had to leave before the game was over, and as I headed for the door someone said, "Hey, Jenkins, aren't you takin' your wife with you?"

To prove I could be just as funny, I pointed at her and said, "No, but I want you home in bed in fifteen minutes."

I was already out the door when I heard the hooting and hollering. I had not intended even to imply anything risqué. I had merely been trying to go along with the joke, and I meant to speak to her as father to daughter, not husband to wife. Of course, everyone took my wanting her home in bed the wrong way, and I knew I would never live it down. In fact, if I tried to go back and explain, no one would believe me.

The girl was sweet and chaste, and the last thing I wanted her to think was that I had been inappropriate and had gotten a laugh at her expense. A hundred feet from the cabin, still hearing the laughter, I knew I had to go back.

When I opened the door, no one even noticed me. Something had happened in the game that had everyone's attention. I was glad to see that Miss Jenkins wasn't sitting there weeping with her head in her hands. When I called her name and she looked up, so did everyone else, and the snickering began again.

"Could I see you for a minute?" I asked, and the room fell silent.

I'll never forget her response. "I'm not too sure," she said.

It was the funniest comeback I could imagine, and I wish I'd anticipated it. Even if my original line *had* been intentional, hers was better.

The place erupted again. I was grateful when she bounced to her feet and followed me out into the darkness. I had the impression she knew what I was going to say.

"You need to know that I didn't mean that the way it sounded," I said.

"I know," she said.

"You do?"

"Of course."

"I don't think anyone else understands that."

"Maybe not, but I do. I've seen you around, heard you be funny. That's not your style."

"Your comeback was priceless," I said.

"I couldn't pass it up."

"Anyway, I'm sorry," I said. "I didn't mean to embarrass you."

"Accepted," she said. "And I'm sorry, too, though I *did* mean to embarrass you."

I laughed, and she added, "We Jenkinses have to stick together, you know."

I learned to be more careful about teasing in a flirtatious manner. I also learned how wonderful and forgiving and insightful some people can be. Funny, too.

By the Same Token

Along these same lines, I have made it a practice not to make my wife the butt of jokes. There are enough things to make fun of and enough funny topics without going for easy laughs at the expense of my spouse.

One of the reasons for this is that I would never want Dianna to think I was trying to tell her something serious under the guise of humor. We have established a policy to speak honestly and forthrightly with each other about anything that bothers us.

We give the lie to the charge that married couples who never fight are probably as miserable and phony as those who fight all the time. We love each other. We don't always agree, and we get on each other's nerves occasionally, but neither of us likes tension in the air. We compete to see who can apologize first and get things talked out. We follow the biblical injunction to never let the sun go down on our wrath (see Ephesians 4:26).

When a group of adult Christian couples decides it would be healthy to be honest and to share some of their most embarrassing or petty fights, we always confess that we'll either have to pass or make one up. Slammed doors, cold shoulders, silent treatments, and walking out are just not part of our routine. This comes as a result of being careful with our tongues.

Just as I don't want to make the mistake of flirting in jest or being suggestive in conversation with anyone but my wife, I try to watch what I say to her, too. Scripture has a lot to say about the power of the tongue and the spoken word. Proverbs 18:21 says that "death and life are in the power of the tongue," and Proverbs 21:23 says, "Whoever guards his mouth and tongue keeps his soul from troubles."

Proverbs 28:23 says, "He who rebukes a man will find more favor afterward than he who flatters with the tongue." In the New Testament, James said that "the tongue is a little member and boasts great things. See how great a forest a little fire kindles!" (James 3:5).

Flattery, flirtation, suggestive jesting, and what we say to our own spouses are all shades of the same color. Beware the power of the tongue.

13

LOOKING BACK

Hedge No. 5. I remind my wife often, in writing and orally, that I remember my wedding vows, especially this one: "Keeping you only unto me for as long as we both shall live."

If, following the so-called free love movement of the previous century, it seemed that living together or practicing open marriage had superseded traditional, biblical marriage, the twenty-first century has brought even more revolution. Marriage has become de rigueur among homosexuals, and campaigns abound to relegitimize plural marriage and even what's referred to as polyamory. Believe it or not, the latter has become alarmingly evident even in some evangelical churches. While it may not be widely promoted aloud, I've had pastors tell me that they hear of it and see it among parishioners who challenge them to prove that it in any way violates Scripture.

What Is Polyamory?

Often abbreviated as *poly*, it is simply a form of consensual non-monogamy in which people practice multiple romantic or intimate relationships at the same time. Proponents maintain that, with the knowledge and consent of all parties, these relationships are based on and thrive on communication, trust, and what they often refer to as "ethical behavior."

Despite the clear teachings of the New Testament on monogamy, polyamorists insist that they're hurting no one and that they're "more honest" than traditional marriage partners who cheat on each other.

At the risk of simplicity, the very idea of polyamorism should be thrown out with the trash as we simply remind our wives and ourselves of the sacred vow we affirmed before God and others at our weddings: "Keeping you only unto me for as long as we both shall live."

What Does the Bible Say about This?

In Matthew 19:4-6, Jesus cited God's idea from the book of Genesis that "a man shall leave his father and mother and be joined to his wife, and the two shall become one flesh." In 1 Timothy 3:2 and Titus 1:6, a list of qualifications for church leaders requires that they be "the husband of one wife."

People seem to take their wedding vows so cavalierly nowadays that you have to wonder if they have any idea what they're saying. Nearly a hundred years ago, US census figures showed that one of every four marriages performed between 1931 and 1933 ended in divorce. The *National Affairs* publication "The Evolution of Divorce" discusses the divorce rate in the 1950s. It states that in 1950, less than 20 percent of couples got divorced. By 1970, about 50 percent of couples who married did, and about half the children born to married parents in the 1970s had divorced parents.[1]

Several decades ago, according to the *Barna Update* of September 2004, among all adults who had been married, 35 percent had also been divorced, and 3 percent were presently separated. Eighteen percent of adults who had ever been divorced had been divorced more than once.[2]

Barna updated their research four years later, reporting that most Americans get married at some point in their life: Just one out of five adults (22 percent) had never been married. Among those who had married, one of three had divorced at least once. Barna revealed that an even higher proportion of Christians (84 percent) marry. They said that among the population with the least likelihood of divorcing were Catholics (28 percent), evangelicals (26 percent), upscale adults (22 percent), Asians (20 percent), and those who considered themselves conservatives (28 percent).[3]

So Where Does This Stand Today?

According to Wilkinson and Finkbeiner, divorce and family law attorneys based in San Diego and Coronado, California, the current divorce rate is nearly double that of 1960, but down from the all-time high of 22.6 percent in the early 1980s. Their research shows that almost 50 percent of all marriages in the United States will end in divorce or separation and that 41 percent of all first marriages end in divorce.

But get this: Wilkinson and Finkbeiner have also said that 60 percent of second marriages end in divorce, and 73 percent of all third marriages end in divorce.[4]

It may be naïve to think that people would remain true to their vows just by repeating them frequently, but who knows? At least couples might come to really understand what they said in a ceremony before God, friends, and spouse. Is it possible that couples reciting their vows in Elizabethan or modern language truly have not thought through what they're saying? "I will keep you only unto me

> People seem to take their wedding vows so cavalierly nowadays that you have to wonder if they have any idea what they're saying.

for as long as we both shall live" means "I won't sleep with anyone
else." Maybe that would sound crude in a wedding ceremony, but it
might be less likely to be forgotten.

Practical Suggestions

You can use many creative ways to remind your spouse and yourself of your wedding vows, and those ways can be adapted to any
budget. For example, try surprising your wife with a progressive
search that culminates in a trip somewhere special. If you can
afford it, take her out of the country. If you can't, drive to the next
town for a weekend at a hotel. Or even just to McDonald's.

Set it up this way: Write out slips that contain your wedding
vows, particularly those that refer to remaining sexually faithful, in
a rhyme or even a short-story format. At the end of each slip, leave
a clue that leads to where your wife can find the next one. Then
hide them around the house and in the garage.

Mail the first one home. It might say, "Keeping you—" and
then "Look for another message in the freezer."

When she looks in the freezer, she finds another slip that reads,
"—only unto me—" and "Look for another message in the car."

In the car is a slip that reads, "—for as long—" and points her
to the mantel over the fireplace. There she finds a note that says,
"—as we both—" and "Look for another message in the junk
drawer." There she will find a message that reads, "—shall live."
There you might also plant a plane ticket or hotel reservation or
babysitting certificate or restaurant gift certificate.

It can be just as effective, though maybe not as much fun,
simply to call her at home or at work, and tell her, "I made this vow
__ years/months/days ago, and I still mean it: 'I will keep you only
unto myself for as long as we both shall live, or until Christ, who
has saved us by His grace, returns to take us unto Himself forever.'"

Sending your vows in snail mail can be unique and effective.
Email and texting are a little too easy and cheap, but they're better

than nothing and probably how you communicate daily. You might even have someone pen your vows in calligraphy or have them printed so you can frame them. I've heard of people having their vows written in icing on a cake, chiseled into a rock, burned into wood, and even furrowed in moist dirt in the front yard. A friend of mine spent a couple of hours forming the letters to his vows in tiny bits of twig and then set them up on the cement slab in front of the door of his house, only to see his wife miss their significance and sweep them off the porch onto the grass.

Sometimes I like to just tell Dianna that I remember my vows and that she is the only woman I have ever slept with, and the only one I ever wish to sleep with. I usually add my own sentiments on anniversary and birthday cards too. I don't think she ever tires of hearing me reiterate my vows. I know I never get tired of hearing or saying them.

What's Good for the Goose

The sad fact is that there is simply not enough emphasis on wedding vows anymore. We need to face it: This is one of the most significant problems in modern marriage. I've never understood the long-standing double standard that seems to wink at males' infidelity while holding women in contempt for the same offense. Of course, the breaking of a sacred vow should not be tolerated for either sex, but there is an insidious boys-will-be-boys mentality that allows some men—even Christians—to have occasional or long-standing mistresses their entire married lives.

As we've seen countless marriages break up during our half century together, Dianna and I have talked seriously about this issue. *Divorce* is not in our vocabulary, but we have discussed how difficult it would be—and seemingly impossible in our flesh—to forgive the other for the ultimate in unfaithfulness and betrayal.

I will say, however, that both our views have grown on this subject. We have seen friends' and relatives' marriages shattered by adultery, and yet we have also counseled spouses to forgive each other and take each other back. Regaining trust after adultery still seems impossible, but there are other things to consider.

For instance, we have seen that adultery is usually not the major problem in bad marriages. It is more often the *result* of a bad marriage or the *symptom* of a bad marriage. It may be the worst thing that can happen to a sacred union, but it is rarely the root problem. We hope and trust and believe and pray that any of our discussions about this subject are academic in our own marriage because we work so hard at it, but adultery does occasionally invade even seemingly solid marriages. That's the whole reason for this book.

Take the case of a Christian leader who stepped down from an executive position with a mission organization after his adultery was revealed. His wife, his pastor, and a couple of close relatives already knew of his sin, and also of his repentance. When it came to light, however, he realized that resigning was the only way to protect the reputation of the mission and keep it from extended controversy.

> Adultery may be the worst thing that can happen to a sacred union, but it is rarely the root problem.

Anyone who knew this man knew he had been a model husband and father. Even his wife and children said so. Thus, the shocking moral lapse was clearly not the result of a pattern in his life or of a bad marriage. He admitted that during a period of burnout and extreme fatigue, he allowed a friendship to become immoral, and he apparently sincerely repented.

Most interesting was that his wife not only forgave him but also said that she would not dwell on his short period of unfaithfulness. To their credit, neither discounted that he had sinned, that his actions were unacceptable, or that he needed to repent and ask for forgiveness from God and all affected individuals. Some feel he has forever disqualified himself from the ministry, but my purpose here is to deal with the forgiveness aspect.

If he was truly repentant, did his wife have a choice as a Christian to do anything but forgive him and welcome him back? Whereas many believe that adultery is biblical grounds for divorce, surely divorce is not mandated when the offending party is remorseful and wants to reconcile.

Clearly the biblical, Christian response to a repentant sinner is forgiveness. In ourselves, in our flesh, this would probably not be possible. Only through Christ can divine, unconditional love find forgiveness for a spouse who has foisted the filthiest pollution on a marriage.

One thing is certain: Marriages in which the ultimate loss of trust has been suffered can never be the same. We can only imagine what a wife who has taken back a husband who slept with another woman, or vice versa, must go through when that offending spouse wants to enjoy the marriage bed again. How long would it be—if ever—before either could forget that the vows had been broken, that one of them had not kept the other only unto himself or herself? Could deep, abiding trust ever be fully regained? No wonder few marriages survive such an onslaught.

Even considering that jumble of horrifying emotions is so distasteful that all it does is make me want to emphasize again the whole reason for this book. Again, I need to say that adultery is usually a result or symptom of a marriage with weaknesses throughout. If protecting your marriage requires occasionally imagining being caught or having to confess to your wife that you've been unfaithful, then I recommend that exercise.

You won't find it pleasant. Imagine breaking down as you tell her, hoping she'll understand, seeing her turn away cold and hurt, not wanting to be touched or to hear any more. My guess is that the typical woman won't want to see her husband's tears of grief and remorse right away. He will tumble off whatever pedestal he may have been on, and should she ever find it within herself, by the grace of God, to forgive him and take him back, it will not be without deep pain and suffering.

Imagine, just imagine, what that would do to your wife. Plant hedges wide and deep and tall against any weakness you may have. Remind yourself what price you would have to pay for a brief season of carnal fun. Study what is wrong within you or in your relationship with your wife that would allow you to even consider such a drastic breach of her trust.

Dianna and I had college friends who had been married for ten years and had two sons when we first got wind there was trouble. The wife suspected her husband was seeing another woman. We stood by her, helped her find out, confronted him, heard the denials, and then learned the awful truth: It was true.

He was unrepentant, hostile, and flagrant. He had complaints about his wife, but none justified this complete setting aside of his morals and values. She kept fighting for him, wanting him back. We warned her that until he gave up the other woman and—in essence—came back on his knees, she should be slow to open her arms. Maybe we were intruding rather than helping, but she received similar counsel from others.

Still, she was desperate. She couldn't stand the thought of losing him to someone else. No, she was not the woman he had married. She had given birth to both sons within a year of each other, and she had grown weary and harried trying to keep up with them. Maybe she had become shrill, and maybe she had neglected him, but he had never grown up either. Now he played most of the time and was gone more than he was home. And now this—another woman.

She moved in with her aunt and took the boys with her. He begged her to come back, promising to change his ways. It was all she wanted to hear. She set conditions: "Give up the other woman, spend time at home, don't expect Olympic sex after this rupture of my trust, and grow up."

The first night they spent together again, he got a call from the other woman. "Take that call and I'm out of here," his wife told him.

"Just some loose ends," he assured her, and they talked on the phone for half an hour. Then he left. "Just getting some stuff, settling accounts. Don't worry. It's over."

He was gone all night and still tried to tell her nothing had happened. But he had pushed his wife past the brink. She packed up the boys and all her belongings and moved out. Even while he was again pleading with her to take him back, a friend saw his car in front of his girlfriend's house all night. The friend left a note, berating him for living a lie. That finally brought him to his senses.

From what we could tell, he had finally truly repented. He'd come back to God, cut off the relationship, and done everything he could to win back his wife.

But it was too late. Had his wife been Jesus, she might have forgiven him seventy times seven, and there were those who felt she was being cold and unforgiving and even unchristian when she didn't. Sadly, he had pushed her too far. I'm not saying she was right, but she got to the place of rage, and suddenly she could believe nothing he said and could trust nothing he promised. She could only be suspicious of everything he did.

Both partners have been married again. She has divorced for the second time.

We're talking about Christian people. Adultery creates chaos. Adulterers lie. Victims get angry. There are human limits to forgiveness, even among Christians.

Somehow, some way, we who have remained true to our spouses need to do something to ensure we continue that way. That means working on our weaknesses, shoring up our strengths, pouring our lives into each other, and planting hedges like regularly reciting our vows to each other. We must avoid the mess of adultery and divorce and the besmirching of the reputation of Christ. The time is long past for us to worry about people snickering at us for being prudish or Victorian or puritanical.

Treat this blight on marriage as the epidemic it is. Flee. Plant a hedge. Do something. Anything. Don't become a sad statistic.

14

LOVE IS SPELLED T-I-M-E

Hedge No. 6. From the time I got home from work until the children went to bed, I did no writing or other work. That gave me lots of time daily with the family and for my wife and me to continue to court and date.

I render this hedge in past tense because my present family is vastly different. Naturally, our three sons—all in their forties at this writing—are grown and gone, so I have changed my sixth hedge to the one about accountability I outlined in chapter 2. That's one you don't need to wait to plant until you're older. I wish I'd thought of it years ago. It's important to me at this age, and fortunately I was accountable to my superiors back when I was working, and of course to my church leadership. But an accountability board for yourself can prove valuable at any age. I'll say a bit more about that later.

Now, my original hedge, featured in this chapter, may have been the best and most valuable of them all. Let me explain how it came about.

Something subtle but unusual happened after Dianna and I had been married for about a year. I had recently left the field of secular journalism and had begun working for Scripture Press Publications. Among my duties was interviewing people for stories for Sunday school handouts.

Coincidentally, several of my interviews during a short span were with men about twice the age I was then. I was in my early twenties, so they were in their midforties.

Their stories were all different, but eventually we got around to the subjects of home and marriage and family, and I asked each if he had any regrets at this stage of his life. Every one said he wished he'd spent more time with his kids during their growing-up years. Their marriages had been fine, and their children had turned out okay, but they all mentioned a lot of "if onlys."

"If only I'd realized my daughter's recital was more important than the big real estate deal . . ."

"If only I could have proved to my son how proud I was of him by showing up at his games . . ."

"If only my wife had known before she died how much I enjoyed talking with her and traveling with her . . ."

It's become a cliché by now that no one has ever been heard to say on his deathbed, "I wish I'd spent more time working."

These expressions of regret over misplaced priorities during the sunny years of their careers—which always seem to coincide with the growing-up years of a man's family—had little to do with their stories and didn't wind up in the pages of Scripture Press's Sunday school papers. But I sensed God had put me in contact with these men because He was trying to tell me something: If I had those same regrets at their age, I would be without excuse.

> Every one said he wished he'd spent more time with his kids during their growing-up years.

I remember a lengthy discussion with Dianna about this. We wouldn't have our first child until we'd been married four and a half years, so that gave us a lot of time to set goals, policies, and priorities. We wanted to be good parents and avoid regrets.

We decided that once children came along, I would do no writing and no office business between the time I got home from work and the time the kids went to bed. (I've been accused of sometimes putting them to bed at 4:30 p.m.)

In the beginning, the biggest benefit was to Dianna. She had someone to take over feeding and changing and entertaining a baby while she finally had time to herself. Sometimes baby Dallas was sleeping when I got home, but that didn't count; he had to be down for the night before I felt free to get into my own projects.

When Chad came along two and a half years later, Dallas had already learned to take for granted that I would be around during that time of the day. I didn't insist that the boys honor the time I had carved out for them or even that they interact with me. I just wanted them to get used to the fact that I was theirs to talk to, to play with, or even to ignore.

I learned that a popular idea of that day was a lie. Some experts advised that successful overachievers could be guilt free about the little time they were able to devote to their children if only they invested *quality* time when they could. It was sort of like one-minute parenting. Just be sure that what little time you're able to spend with your child is quality time.

What garbage!

I've seen the results of kids who were given only so-called quality time. The problem is that kids don't know the difference. What they need is time—all they can get. Quantity time is quality time, whether you're discussing the meaning of the cosmos or just climbing on Dad.

There were times I wished my kids knew how wonderful I was being about all this. I didn't know many fathers who gave their kids at least two and a half hours a day—and there certainly weren't any other fathers who played ball with the whole neighborhood every summer evening.

But of course this was not all just for the kids' benefit. Looking back, I can't imagine missing their growth experiences or the funny and touching things they said, and even having been there in times of crisis when I could easily have been somewhere else.

One time Dallas, at about age four, told me he wished he had a new dad. That pierced me, because I thought I was a pretty good dad. But I covered and asked, "Like who?"

"Like the man down the street," he said. I knew exactly who he was talking about and why.

The man down the street came home so infrequently that he got a royal welcome every time he did. And he was usually feeling so guilty about his drinking, topless barhopping, or compulsive spending that he brought gifts for everyone. What a guy! What a dad! He must be super to get that kind of reception and be so generous!

I couldn't explain the distinctions to Dallas until he was old enough to understand why the man down the street left his wife a note one morning telling her she would find his body in the closed garage with the car running.

So What?

What does all this have to do with marital hedges? Hedges can do wonders for a family, and this policy of spending mega-blocks of time with the kids each day turned into rich benefits for Dianna and me too. Our time together was more relaxed, less hurried, less pressured, less obligatory. We learned to just be with each other, to be used to having each other around. We didn't have to talk, plan, schedule, or make appointments with each other. We knew each other's schedules, and we counted on when the other would be available.

Dianna tells me she enjoyed a tremendous sense of satisfaction and well-being when I was devoting time to the kids. She never felt left out or jealous, especially since she and I also spent a lot of time together.

A Rose by Any Other Name

I was reminded of how important the strength of a marriage is to children when I saw a quote from Pete Rose Jr. The betting scandal his baseball-star father got caught in meant little to Petey. But he still, as a young adult, dwelt on his parents' years-old divorce. His father was remarried with a new child and another on the way. His mother was tending bar in Cincinnati.

Petey was a better-than-average big-league prospect himself, and athletes at that stage in their careers are usually single-minded and driven. Yet Petey said something like this: "I would trade whatever future I have in big league baseball to see my parents get back together."[1]

It was as if he hadn't read the papers and didn't know the truth about his parents' marriage. Pete Sr. had a reputation for womanizing, and such nasty, impossible-to-take-back things had been said by each of Petey's parents about the other that there was no possibility of civility, let alone reconciliation. And with Pete Sr. remarried, there was no chance.

Yet that comment from little Pete, if he were my son, would haunt me to my grave. The fact is, that's a common theme from adult children of divorce.

Love Me, Love My Mom

The following statement has been attributed to everybody from Howard Hendricks to Josh McDowell to James Dobson. It probably preceded all three, but it remains true: "The most important thing a father can do for his children is to love their mother."

When we understand that one of the great fears of childhood is abandonment, we can only imagine the impact of a broken marriage on a child.

May "the Vorce" Not Be with You

Some things never seem to change. As I mentioned, the first itera-
tion of this book was released more than three decades ago, and yet
it seems more needed now than ever. I didn't want to fill this version with outdated data and resources,
yet as I have painstakingly researched
current trends, I find them depress-
ingly similar to, or worse than, the
data back then.

> When we understand that
> one of the great fears of
> childhood is abandonment,
> we can only imagine the
> impact of a broken marriage
> on a child.

As far back as 1978, *Campus Life*
magazine ran a story about "the vorce,"
which represented a child's misunderstanding of the word *divorce*. A child
in the story said that sometimes people
even talk about "the the vorce," which she couldn't understand at
all. All she knew was that anytime anyone ever talked about "the
vorce" or "the the vorce," it was sad and bad news. It had something
to do with Mommy and Daddy, and she didn't like the vorce.[2]

It reminded me of a little girl I knew when I was seven. I
thought she was the sweetest, cutest four-year-old I had ever seen.
Because of our difference in age, I didn't see much of her during
the next few years. But by the time she was nine, she was a sad
little creature with a drawn face and red eyes. The only thing she
would tell her Sunday school teacher was that she was afraid of
the vorce. Her teacher thought she meant some kind of force, but
soon the truth came out.

Her parents were leaders in the church and seemed to have an
idyllic family with several children, including a couple of adoptees.
More than once, however, the children had been awakened in the
night by their parents' arguing, even yelling and screaming. That
was when this pretty little girl had first heard about the vorce.
Her mother was pleading with her father not to get the vorce.
Whatever it was, the little girl knew it was bad.

Divorcees—and frankly, many websites today—will tell you that children are resilient, that a divorce is better for a child than a bad marriage. But real experts in child psychology tell a different story, as they have been doing for decades. And if you are an adult survivor of your parents' divorce when you were a child, you know they're right.

Some kids who bottle up their emotions and pretend it's all right to be shuttled back and forth between parents and cities, often by plane, grow up to be emotional wrecks. They struggle to trust or fully love anyone. They often fear rejection, suffer low self-esteem, career in and out of their own doomed marriages, and leave in their wakes children just like themselves.

Donna Kato, in her article "Children Suffer More from Divorce Than Previously Thought" from a few years before the turn of the century, cited a study coauthored by family expert Judith Wallerstein and San Francisco State University professor Julia Lewis, which looked at 130 children aged two to six from sixty families. They studied and interviewed the children at intervals that ranged from every eighteen months to five years, and Wallerstein reached several conclusions, including: "Divorce affects children psychologically, economically, and socially. Half of the young people in the study became involved in serious drug and alcohol abuse, many before the age of 14."[3]

Another landmark study found that nine of ten children of divorce suffered a sense of shock at the separation, "including profound grieving and irrational fears."[4] Half reported feelings of rejection and abandonment.[5] And 37 percent were more "unhappy and dissatisfied five years after the divorce than they had been at 18 months."[6]

As I said, many of these conclusions originated with studies from years ago. So how does that research stack up with what's going on today? FamilyMeans, a multiservice nonprofit, recently reported its findings on the impact of divorce on children.[7] Among the effects:

- *Poor performance in academics.* The more distracted children are, the more likely they are to be unable to focus on their schoolwork.
- *Loss of interest in social activity.* Sometimes children feel insecure and wonder if their family is the only family that has gotten divorced.
- *Difficulty adapting to change.* Children can be affected by new family dynamics, living situations, schools, friends, and more.
- *Emotional sensitivity.* Feelings of loss, anger, confusion, and anxiety may come from this transition, leaving children feeling overwhelmed.
- *Anger/irritability.* Though for many children this anger dissipates after several weeks, it may be a lingering effect.
- *Feelings of guilt.* Children often wonder whether they have done something wrong, which can lead to depression, stress, and other health problems.
- *Introduction of destructive behavior.* Research has shown that children who have experienced divorce in the previous twenty years were more likely to participate in crimes and destructive behavior, like smoking or prescription drug abuse.
- *Increase in health problems.* Children who have experienced divorce have a higher perceptibility to sickness, which can stem from many factors, including difficulty going to sleep.
- *Loss of faith in marriage and the family unit.* Children of divorce naturally wonder, *What's the point of getting married if it's going to end in such chaos?*

While I knew perhaps a couple of kids from broken homes when I was in elementary school, by now it's not unusual to find that as many as half the students in even a Christian school have different last names from their parents. Imagine what their family reunions and family trees look like. These kids will one day run our corporations, lead our government, and pioneer technological progress.

We can grow paranoid, I guess, but with divorce wreaking havoc on the minds and emotions of so many children, mayhem seems the only prognosis. The only way to ensure a future with stable marriages and home lives is to begin strengthening our families now. Give kids a model of love and caring and interdependence. Show them what it means to make and keep a commitment, to set your course on a lifetime of love with no wavering, no excuses, and no me-first philosophies.

Don't fall prey to the "quality time" trap or to the myth that kids are resilient and will be better off in two halves of a broken home. Most children of divorce are just like Pete Rose Jr. They'd give up everything else in their lives if only their parents would get back together. Make a decision. Set a course. Carve out the time it takes to devote yourself to your wife and children, and plant a hedge that will protect you, her, and them from the devastation of a broken home.

PART THREE

FAMILY BENEFITS

When you tell your story, speak openly of the hedges in your marriage, protect yourself and your family from insidious new sources of unacceptable media, and truly practice the Golden Rule at home, it will give your spouse and your children a deep sense of love and security.

15

LOVE'S TAPESTRY

It's important to share with your spouse and children the memories of your own courtship, marriage, and honeymoon. And it's never too late to recall the memories of your early love. The longer you go without doing it, the easier it is to forget important details. But by telling your story over and over through the years, you solidify in your mind the things that attracted you to your mate in the first place. Just as important, your children learn the history of the relationship.

I was always fascinated by the stories my parents told about how they met, fell in love, and stayed true to each other during their engagement, although World War II kept them apart for thirty-four months before they married in 1945.

There are various ways of reminding one another and your children of your own love story. Obviously, it's not a good idea to force the story on casual acquaintances or neighbors—unless they ask—but you'd be surprised by how many people are indeed interested: old friends, close relatives, people from church you know well. Trade stories with them. Everybody loves a love story.

> By telling your story over and over through the years, you solidify in your mind the things that attracted you to your mate in the first place.

I tell my own story here only to show the types of memories you can ferret out to share with your mate and others. I call it *my* own, rather than *our* own, because every courtship is really two stories, yours and your spouse's. Dianna's story contains parallel elements, of course, but the emphases are hers, and her perspective is unique.

Every time we tell our stories, we remind each other of incidents we hadn't thought of since they occurred in the early 1970s. Every birthday, anniversary, holiday, or no-reason-I-just-felt-like-sending-a-card occasion provides an opportunity for a note or a comment, maybe just a sentence from our wedding vows to share with each other. Repeat a wedding vow in your spouse's ear the next time you kiss hello or goodbye. There's no reason not to celebrate your wedding anniversary in some small way every day.

If you have a good marriage, build a hedge around it by celebrating it. Think how unique a gift you have been blessed with in this generation of divorce—and worse, the trend toward no marriage at all.

My Story

I had not dated for a year when a friend and his fiancée began telling me of a girl I just had to meet, a classmate of theirs at Fort Wayne (Indiana) Bible College. She was tall and beautiful, they told me. *Oh, sure, I thought. That's why she has to resort to blind dates.*

I got a look at her from afar when I visited the campus and saw her in the homecoming court. They were right. She was gorgeous.

So much so that I was intimidated. No way would I have dreamed she had a night free, let alone that she would accept a date with me. I'd probably waste my time and pride by asking her out.

"But we've told her about you," my friends said. "She's open to a blind date."

"Forget it," I said. "I've seen her. She hasn't seen me." But my interest was piqued. Maybe someday.

Someday came a few months later. They talked me into driving over from Chicago for a double date. Ever the romantic, I started building the possibilities in my mind. I told myself that if anything was to come from this, I would know immediately and be smitten with her.

The blind date on a Friday night in May 1970 was fine. She was lovely, refined, soft-spoken, smart, likable, and easy to talk to. But there were no whistles, bells, or fireworks. As soon as he got me alone, my friend wanted to know what I thought.

"Fine," I said.

"Just fine?"

I nodded.

"Could you get interested? Try to build something?"

"Nah. I don't know. I don't think so."

"Why? Something wrong?"

"No. We just didn't click."

"You've had one date!"

"Yeah, but I'd know."

"You're crazy."

"Maybe I am."

The next night we doubled again, and my reaction was the same. Dianna and I promised to write, and feeling polite and benevolent, I said maybe I would visit her again. We corresponded occasionally over the next few weeks, and I sensed Dianna was more interested than I was. In fact, if she had not gently reminded me that I had said I would come back, I probably wouldn't have. (Frankly, that lunacy is not something I dwell on.)

Dianna told me later that at the wedding of the friends who had introduced us, she sensed my lack of enthusiasm. I was busy in the wedding party and only really spoke to her as she was leaving. For some reason, just before she got into her car, I touched the tip of her nose and said goodbye. She took it as the only bit of encouragement I had given her.

Before I finally drove back to see her in Fort Wayne on July 18, I had the audacity to tell my friend that if everything went the same as before, I was not going to pursue the relationship. "You're crazy," he said.

This time it would not be a double date. She was going to cook dinner for us at her place, and then we would walk around The Landing, an old section of Fort Wayne. I pulled in the driveway and went to the front door. As I rang the bell, I could see Dianna through the screen, heading for the kitchen.

"Come on in," she said. "I have to catch something on the stove."

She flashed a smile as she hurried past, and something happened to me. After two double dates and a brief chat at our friends' wedding, it was love at fourth sight. Dianna says the only difference since I had seen her last was her tan. That makes me sound pretty shallow, but there it is. I don't know what clicked. All I know is that it was the most dramatic emotion I have ever felt, before or since.

I hardly knew the woman, but I was struck dumb and knew beyond doubt that I would marry her. I don't know how I knew, but I knew it as surely as I knew my own name. I followed her into the kitchen, literally unable to say a word. (Anyone who knows me knows how unique that had to be.) If she had asked me how the drive was, I would have been able to manage only a nod.

Dianna is most comfortable when someone else is carrying the conversation. One of the things she liked about me was that I enjoyed talking, drawing people out. And there I stood, like a dolt.

She acted as if she didn't notice and uncharacteristically chattered about the chicken, the vegetables, the salad. I watched her slice carrots, thinking, *She is going to do this in our home someday. I'll watch her do this for the rest of my life.* I can't explain it; I just knew, and I never wavered.

When I finally spoke, my voice cracked, and I noticed her double take. What an ordeal that meal was! Dianna grew up on a farm and was a 4-H champion cook, so the food was wonderful. But I sat trying to make small talk, all the while hiding my delicious secret: I was going to marry this girl. She had seemed more interested in me than I in her before this point, but now I had shot past her by lightyears.

Dianna and I were impressed by different little things that night. I was impressed that a basically shy girl felt comfortable enough to put her feet up on a chair during the meal. Later, as we strolled through The Landing, holding hands for the first time, she was impressed that I wouldn't let her run to the car when it began to rain. She worried about her naturally curly hair. Nothing could have made her less beautiful to me.

Later we drove to a park in the center of the city, where we walked in the rain. It was one of those nights that nearly every couple has at one time or another. We talked about everything, learned of childhood memories, and quizzed each other on favorite colors, foods, tastes in clothes, books—anything that came to mind. I was in paradise.

After two double dates and a brief chat at our friends' wedding, it was love at fourth sight.

I could hardly contain my secret. I wanted to tell her something, anything, that would alert her to the fact that to me this was much, much more than a typical date or even a new relationship. It made no sense, but I knew to the core of my being that this was it. She would be my wife, and nothing anyone did could change that.

Before I left her at midnight for the two-hour drive back to Chicago, I pretended to be kidding and told her I thought I was already falling in love. She found that funny, and I was glad I hadn't seriously revealed my heart. By the time I got in the car, whether it made sense or not, I was helplessly, wholly in love. I thought I had been in love before, but now I knew better.

All the way to Chicago I sang, whistled, talked to myself, and tried to think of someone, anyone, I could tell. One of my friends worked in an all-night gas station in my hometown. I arrived at two in the morning, grinning from ear to ear. I went into the station and sat on a fifty-five-gallon oil drum, beginning a three-and-a-half-hour rhapsody.

"I want you to be in our wedding," I concluded.

My friend shook his head. "You've got it bad."

I didn't know how right he was until I climbed down off that oil drum at five thirty in the morning and realized I'd been sitting in a quarter inch of motor oil the whole time! It had soaked through my seat and down my pant legs, even into my socks.

With the morning newspaper between me and my car seat, I arrived home at six in the morning and peeked into my parents' bedroom. My mother opened one eye. "You're in love," she said.

She couldn't have paid me a higher compliment. I couldn't get over that it showed, and Mom hadn't even seen the oil yet.

I didn't sleep for a couple of days, but I did start on what would become astronomical phone bills over the next several months. I tried as hard as I could not to let my temporary insanity show through, but I failed. Dianna didn't know what to make of it, and when she visited Chicago one weekend, my secret was out. For the next several months, I tried not to make a fool of myself, and she carefully considered this new friend who had started with such ambivalence but was now racing ahead of her own feelings.

During that period, I discovered the depth of the woman I was convinced would be my wife. Before long, my infatuation matured to true love. By September Dianna shared my feelings, and we began to discuss our future. In November she suggested a two-week moratorium on the relationship. We had known each other such a short time and were talking so seriously of marriage that she wanted to back off for a couple of weeks and sort out her feelings. I was devastated.

I didn't tell Dianna, but I was convinced she was doing this only because it was the type of thing her friends had done. Worse, I dreaded that she would come to her senses and realize she could do much better. I believed that if I ever heard from her again, it would be in the form of a Dear John letter or a phone call suggesting that we should just be friends.

This was, of course, years before Dr. James Dobson's excellent book *Love Must Be Tough*, which advises the waiting party in such a relationship to maintain dignity.[1] Part of me wanted to beg and plead and cry and ask how Dianna could do such a thing to a person willing to crawl in front of her for the rest of her life, licking up dirt so she wouldn't have to step in it. Wouldn't that have been an attractive example of the kind of man a woman wants for a husband?

I resisted the urge to grovel, but I did a lot of tearful walking and praying. In retrospect, I was a sniveling weakling who somehow had enough foresight to keep it to himself. But at the time, I was in genuine turmoil. I believed Dianna was meant for me, that only she could make me happy. I held to the conviction that we were meant to be married.

I had to come to the point with God, however, where I was willing to give her up. I had to get to the place where I conceded that if I truly loved her, I would want what was best for her. And if what was best for Dianna was not me, then that was what I wanted for her. Otherwise, my love was selfish. It wasn't easy. In fact, it was the most difficult ordeal of my life. But after four days of agony, I made that concession. I didn't feel much better, and I didn't want things to turn out that way, but I knew I had done the right thing by being willing to accept it.

That night she called. "Enough of this nonsense," she said. "I miss you. Come when you can."

I drove four hours to see her for half an hour, then drove back home. We were married within three months.

I don't begrudge her the four days she needed. I am glad she didn't need the entire two weeks. I would have been a basket case. Whatever she settled in her mind during those few days has lasted our entire marriage. For whatever grief it caused me then, it has afforded me a wife with no second thoughts.

Peoria

Clearly, that story is of great interest only to those involved, including our children. When they were living at home, they often insisted on hearing it. They liked to hear about the wedding, too, giggling over my father pushing the Play button rather than the Record button on his tape recorder at the worst possible moment during the ceremony. While the pastor exhorted us, we were treated to ten seconds of a business seminar Dad was trying to tape over.

We wrote our own vows, borrowing ideas from friends. We promised each other that we would "keep you only unto me," but rather than the morbid "till death do us part," we used the more hopeful "for as long as we both shall live, or until Christ, who has saved us by His grace, returns to take us unto Himself forever."

I also vowed to make Dianna laugh, which I've tried to accomplish daily for more than five decades. (If I've failed by the end of the day, I sometimes resort to swinging from the chandelier.)

We were married in downstate Illinois and left the next day to drive across the country for a job in Washington state. We spent our first honeymoon night at the Holiday Inn in Peoria. It didn't seem at all funny then, but that gets the biggest smile today when we recount our story.

Now tell *your* story. Tell it to your kids, your friends, your brothers and sisters, but especially to each other. The more your story is implanted in your brain, the more it serves as a hedge against the myriad forces that seek to destroy your marriage. Make your story so familiar that it becomes part of the fabric of your being. It should become a legend shared through the generations as you grow a family tree that defies all odds and boasts marriage after marriage of stability, strength, and longevity.

16

YOUR LEGACY

A healthy marriage contributes to a happy family, if my experience is typical. Dianna calls me *Honey* and I call her *Babe*, but when she or our sons talk about me, they call me Dad. Dianna wouldn't say, "Go ask Honey to come upstairs," or "Go ask my husband." She doesn't even call me "your dad," as many mothers refer to their husbands. I'm just Dad.

Oh, it was embarrassing when Dianna forgot that my lunch bag didn't have to be differentiated from thirty others—as the kids' lunches did—and she wrote *DAD* on it in big, block letters. But I still liked the name. It was my favorite until I became Grandpa. And when great-grands come along, I'll become Papa. I can hardly wait.

I do miss the *Daddy* years when the boys were little, but being called *Dad* reminds me of my own father when he was my age. I tried to play the same role with my boys that he played with his

(I was one of four sons, and Dianna and I have three). He was everything to us. It didn't occur to my brothers and me that he'd been raised without a father until we were grown and had children of our own. We can't imagine having grown up without a father. And I'm sure my brothers marvel, as I do, at what a father he was, considering he had no role model.

My siblings and I have a strange custom to this day. Though we're all relatively outgoing and social-minded, when we brothers get together—even after having not seen each other for months— we seem to take each other in stride. (We live in four separate states, so our get-togethers have to be intentional.) The lack of enthusiasm in our greetings doesn't mean anything. It surprises people who expect my brothers and me to embrace or exult, but that's just something we rarely do.

Yet feelings run deep. I sense as much affection in our casually picking up conversations—and relationships—where they left off as I would in a joyous reception.

Part of that, of course, came from our dad. He was a humorous man and an articulate poet but not overly expressive. *Still waters run deep* and *the strong, silent type* are the clichés. A man's man, a Marine, a police chief—still, he was always polite, soft-spoken, considerate, a gentleman. He didn't consider it old-fashioned to open a door for a woman or to rise when one entered the room. I continue that tradition, which seems to amuse Dianna's and my women friends.

I was with my dad in Chicago once when he opened a door for a stranger. She snarled, "I suppose you think that makes you a gentleman."

"Only if you're a lady," Dad said.

He was often told he was "honest to a fault"—quite a commentary if you think about it. Best of all, he was a one-woman man all his life.

If it's true that the best thing a father can do for his children is to love their mother, my brothers and I had the best thing done for us from the days we were born. Dad was an unabashed romantic and proved his love every day. He was a model in his willingness to scrub floors, change diapers, cook, or do whatever else needed doing when all four boys were home and Mom needed help. He was never too much of a man for that.

He didn't merely tell us what to do. He modeled it.

It's said that we get our first and most lasting image of God from our fathers. That makes me grateful. Grateful that my dad was not an alcoholic. Grateful that he was faithful. Grateful that he was industrious. Grateful that he loved his sons unconditionally and proved it more than once. I'm grateful Dad's priorities were right and uncompromising. Grateful that he cared more about people than things, more about family than money, more about loyalty and integrity than image. He was not perfect like our heavenly Father. But to have half his character is my loftiest dream. To be thought of one day the way my brothers and I think of our dad . . . the only thing he didn't teach me was how to comfortably tell him out loud that I love him. But I did and still do, though he's been in heaven since 2003.

From the Mouths of Babes

My now-obsolete hedge about devoting inviolable time for each child during their growing-up years may be one you'll want to adopt and/or adapt now. Believe me, the benefits will be as much for you as for your kids. Sometimes children can be too good to be true. I know the reverse can also be the case, but let me stay on the positive side.

One of my three sons once told me that the wise men brought Jesus gifts of gold, frankincense, and fur. That was when I first became aware of how priceless are some of the treasures that come from the little ones. If you're raising or have raised children, you will identify with some of the following.

When my eldest, Dallas, was six, my wife and I overheard him giving instructions to one of his tiny soldiers. "You may die in this mission," he said, "but if you're a Christian, you'll go to heaven. In heaven you can ask Jesus for anything you want, and if it's all right with your mom, He'll give it to you."

Chad, when eight, informed me he was going to read the Bible "all the way through." I noticed a tiny-print King James Version in his hand. "That's great, Chad," I said. "How far have you gotten already?"

"Genesis 2:9."

"Wouldn't you rather have a children's Bible, something easier to understand?"

"No," he said. "I memorize out of it for Sunday school. I'll read this."

"It's going to take you a long time."

"Oh, yeah. I'll probably be nine by the time I finish."

A few weeks later, he asked me how old Abel was when he died. "I don't think the Bible tells us that, Chad. Some think he was a young person, maybe even a teenager."

"Hmm," he said. "In my Bible, he lived only eight verses!"

One day I heard him tell his little brother, about three at the time, "Mike, plug in the tape recorder."

"I can't, Chaddy, I can't!"

"Mike, don't you know what it says in the Bible? 'I can do all things through Christ who strengthens me.' You can do anything!"

Neither will I forget the day Chad told me the story of Solomon's life, which his Sunday school class had been studying. "He could have asked God for anything, but he asked for wisdom. Then he got everything else anyway, riches and all that." I nodded. "But then, Dad, you know what happened at the end of his life? He blew it. He lost everything."

"It's a sad story really, isn't it, Chad?"

He looked thoughtful. "Yeah. You'd think out of all those wives, one of 'em would've been a Christian."

A Rich Inheritance

As I reflect on my heritage and the impact my father and mother had on my own marriage, I'm struck by the unspeakable privilege of family legacy. You may not enjoy such a wealth of ancestry or so many fond memories. But if you do, never take them for granted. You'll find yourself more grateful as the years pass. And if your history is more checkered, learn from it, break the cycle—whatever it is—and resolve to build marital and family memories that will last long after you're gone.

My own father's father died when my dad was fourteen months old, so of course he never knew him, and all I know of my paternal grandfather comes from oral histories, letters, and his obituary. As I've said, my dad proved to be a remarkable father despite having not grown up with one himself. He gives the lie to the claim that broken families must result in the same as generations pass. My father's four sons have been richly blessed with long-term marriages (the first three of us all passing the fifty-year mark, and our younger brother not far behind).

We were fortunate to have a godly paternal grandmother and both grandparents on my mother's side. My mother's mother died in her late seventies, but our grandfather lived into his nineties. Losing his wife devastated him, but she had been dying for a long time, and, frankly, her ailments had made her difficult to live with for the last several years. As we stood by her casket, I suggested to him that in some ways, her departure had to be a bit of a relief.

"No," he said. "Difficult as this has been, I miss her and would have welcomed many more years with her, just as she was."

He hadn't meant it as a rebuke, but I felt reproved. His simple statement reminded me that he had vowed to love her in sickness and in health, in good times and bad. He relished fulfilling those vows and would have been willing to endure more for the sake of his lifelong love.

My eldest brother, Jim, and I visited Grandpa near the end of his life, an experience that prompted me to write him later:

Dear Grandpa:

It was good to see you recently, even though when Jim and I walked in, you weren't sure at first which of your relatives we were. I could tell you recognized us as two of your twenty-four grandchildren or fifty-plus great-grandchildren, and we didn't mind your asking, "Which one's your mother?"

Our mother is your fourth child and second daughter, Bonita. I can imagine that at age ninety-two it's hard enough to remember your own seven surviving offspring [who have all passed by now], let alone theirs. I can't imagine that I will ever forget those wonderful times we spent at your huge, old home in Wisconsin when I was a child, but should I be blessed with as many years as you, perhaps I will. Neither can I imagine ever forgetting your investment of time and money to self-publish a collection of the cute things your grands and greats have said over the years. I thought of your special project the other day when Michael, our youngest, who just turned seven, told me that he knew Jesus' name. "It's Amen, right?" he said.

A delight in children has been one of your life's hallmarks. You were never too busy, never too important, never so self-absorbed that you couldn't hold one on your knee and giggle at his antics. You loved to see the little ones learn to walk, and now you're justifiably proud that you are one of the few in the nursing home who can get to the dining room on his own. The voice is weak, the gait is deliberate, and the memory is not what it was. But that sly smile, that glint in the eye, tells me it's still you.

I've always appreciated your sweet, gentle spirit and your deep love and interest in your friends and family. You might be surprised to know how much I brag about your creative genius. I'd love to play Scrabble with you or hear you play one of the many musical instruments you invented and so enjoyed performing.

I was surprised to see how strong and clear your handwriting is, especially after you wrote that you are gradually getting weaker. It saddened me that you wrote, "Really, I would like to go to sleep and forget to wake up," but I can certainly understand. I'm sure it feels as if your most important and productive days are over. Perhaps you're bored now with what seems to be simply biding time.

Rest assured that if you do forget to wake up some morning, you'll be sorely missed by more people than you can imagine. Meanwhile, those of us who love you don't begrudge you the wish to see again your son, your wife, and—for the first time— your Savior face to face. We love you so much and will miss you so much that we selfishly want you to stay with us forever. But we ask only that you have as much faith and confidence now in the sovereignty of God and in His timing as you had when you trusted Him for your salvation and for the guiding of your stellar life.

We usually are hesitant to raise the subject of your preceding us to heaven, but of course, we all wonder every time we see you whether it will be the last time. I hope not, but should that be the case, I'll see you at one of the twelve gates of pearl.

Love,
Your grandson Jerry

Reflecting on my grandfather's heritage, and what a model his marriage was, prompted me to write to my own son Dallas a few years later:

Dear Dallas:

It's fun to see a relationship budding. You have discovered someone who cares about you, and vice versa, and so now you have a huge responsibility not only to each other but also to each other's loved ones. I've always admired your standards, and now they will be put to the test. Her family and your family love her and you, but as you progress there are two unknown, unnamed, and probably unrevealed people you should be thinking about just as conscientiously.

I'm referring to your respective future spouses. I know your relationship is embryonic, but as you enjoy getting to know each other better, you may very well start thinking about your future together. You will give no greater gift to her and to her eventual husband than that she enter her marriage a woman of pure character and control—not just physically a virgin but also pure of thought and word and action.

What may in time seem to you sincere expressions of love and affection should be seen in the light of the future. How you talk to each other, what you dwell on, what you watch and read and say and even joke about should be things that honor God and become wonderful memories of a special relationship.

Most of all, your relationship should leave each of you with no regrets: nothing you would be ashamed to take with you into marriage. The odds are very much against the prospect of your marrying someone you dated as a teenager. That's why my emphasis is on your future spouses, given the probability that they will not be the two of you.

You know that I was involved in a lengthy relationship and was even engaged to be married before we broke up and eventually married other people. How grateful I am for the provision of God, the purity of that woman, and the way we complemented and counteracted (as appropriate) each other's strengths and weaknesses.

I haven't seen my former fiancée for more than two decades, yet I would be able to look her and her husband in the eye and be proud that we did nothing we had to regret or hide from our spouses. That required strategy, foresight, planning, and care. We heard enough, cared enough, and knew enough to stay out of situations that would test our will power past reasonable limits.

At some point you will soon start imagining, wondering, contemplating, toying with the idea that you might indeed become each other's future spouse. It happens. All the more reason to follow the above advice. Think of your future spouses all the time, even if they are you. Don't fall into thinking, "Hey, it's going to be just the two of us forever anyway," as if that justifies anything.

As I say, the odds are against that happening, but if that is God's will, you'll have given each other the greatest wedding present anyone can give: pure minds and bodies and hearts and consciences, having proved your dedication to God on the tempting battlefield of real life.

Your greatest advantage is that you come from families who care deeply about such matters and aren't afraid to talk about them. All four parents will be honored and thrilled if you stand with that ever-shrinking minority that goes against the grain and does the right thing because it's the right thing. No excuses, no alibis, no rationalization, no pointing the finger and saying, "Everybody does it," no easy ways out.

There are reasons for God's clear prohibitions in the area of sexual purity, and as with every biblical restriction, the payoffs for obedience are that much more rewarding than any temporary pleasure. May you maintain your standards. We love you with all our hearts and want only the best for you. And may you do the same for the one you care about, because she is no less loved by her family.

Love,
Dad

As with every biblical restriction, the payoffs for obedience are that much more rewarding than any temporary pleasure.

Interestingly, at least to me, is that Dallas did not marry the girl he was going with at that time. Rather, God led him to Amanda, the woman who proved perfect for him. Hard as it is for Dianna and me to imagine, they recently celebrated their twenty-fifth anniversary.

Son Chad met his bride, Christa, a few years later, and they're already closing in on twenty years of marriage at the time of this writing.

Mike is still looking but enjoys being an uncle eight times over.

Planting hedges can result in a legacy of beautiful marriages— yes, even in the crazy world we live in today.

17

DISCIPLINE, CONSISTENCY, VICTORY, TOTALITY

The title of this chapter comes from a plaque on the wall of a college friend back in the 1960s. I have no idea where it originated, but obviously it has stuck with me. It strikes me that it applies to this idea of planting hedges around my mind, my heart, my hands, and my marriage. If I can remain consistent with this discipline, I will see victory in fleeing lust, which results in a pure and happy marriage. Could there be a better definition of *totality*?

That's one of the reasons I have adjusted my sixth hedge from devoting time to the kids when they were growing up to now being sure I hold myself accountable to someone in all areas of life. For many years I was accountable to my superiors and, of course, to the leadership of the churches we've attended. But when I moved to full-time freelance writing, I became my own boss.

Naturally, I am accountable to my wife and remain accountable to church leadership. But I also feel the need to answer to a small group of men whom I trust and who I know will be honest with me. My little accountability team comprises three dear friends of more than a quarter century. They are of a similar vintage as I am—one slightly older, one slightly younger, and one virtually the same age. One is a retired pastor, one a businessman, one self-employed. We see each other when we can, but we interact formally monthly via Zoom. With them I can truly be myself. It isn't that I'm deceptive with all others, but we do tend to put our best foot forward when relationships are at risk, don't we?

Having to be on our best behavior most of the time isn't all bad. But at times I need to relax, tell somebody everything, revert to adolescence, and enjoy a relationship built on years of trust and confidence. Where else—outside my family—can I sing aloud to oldies on the radio, laugh till I cry, recall childish pranks with humor rather than embarrassment, and be myself, warts and all? We all tease that we each have enough knowledge about each other to ruin our respective reputations. Ours are friendships that endure, that pick up where they leave off.

Though separated by hundreds of miles (we live in Colorado, Illinois, Michigan, and Florida), we have been "together" through job changes, moves, disappointments, heartaches, and joys. When I think of these men, I'm reminded of a conversation I had with the crusty old publisher of the first newspaper I worked for. He once mentioned that he had a twenty-five-year friendship. He must have noticed my blank expression. At barely nineteen, I didn't understand the significance.

"How many people do you know," he asked, "who have had the same friend for that long? Someone who's not related?"

He had a point.

"Someday," he added, "you'll realize how rare it is to have a friend for that long."

My accountability board and I have stood the test of time.

My challenge to you is to cultivate friendships, ones that will last and bear the weight of mutual accountability. I covet a friendship or two like that for you, ones that could last if you make sure they do. Friendships like that are between people who can be honest with each other, laugh at each other's faults, and don't try to change one another—unless intervention is necessary. Best friends are loyal and care and can keep confidences. Best friends can argue and disagree and even raise their voices at each other without worrying an iota about the future of the relationship.

> At times I need to relax, tell somebody everything, revert to adolescence, and enjoy a relationship built on years of trust and confidence.

Best friendships develop roots. We know each other's histories from the time we met. I can mention a name or a situation that might take an hour to explain to someone else, and each knows exactly what I'm talking about. We can speak in shorthand in public, making plans and speaking in code about how we need to get going, while the people around us think we're merely gabbing.

We can tell each other things no one else would dare tell us— bad breath, a runny nose, collar sticking up, shirttail hanging out, talking too loudly, saying the wrong thing.

"That wasn't really funny."

"Oh, yeah? Drop dead."

"You never have been able to beat me at this game."

"Oh, I am so sure."

Best friends are long past the point of thinking they have no faults. Knowing each other well and still caring about each other is what makes best friends. Best friends aren't made overnight. It takes years.

You don't get to have a woman as a best friend, unless she's your wife. It just doesn't work any other way. There's no future in it, no matter what exceptions you hear about or dream about.

And while I'm urging you to cultivate a best friend and even an accountability board, don't ever let those relationships come *between* you and your wife. In truth, when it comes to my group of closest friends, our wives love to see us get together. They're not threatened by our friendships or even the time it sometimes takes. Our friendships are good for our marriages because we admonish and encourage and caution each other.

Some friendships, huh? May you develop some just like them.

Examples

Something wonderful happens in a relationship when hedges begin to grow. It's crucial to understand that the hedges I've discussed have been my own, tailor-made for an oversexed, gregarious, fun-loving, busy person who might otherwise follow his lusts, say things he shouldn't, flirt, forget the most important person in his life, and not spend as much time with his family as he should.

The important thing is to know yourself, understand the dangers in your weak areas, and do something practical and concrete about them.

Your weaknesses may be different. Some might make me laugh or make me think you're a nut, as some of mine may have done to you. The important thing is to know yourself, understand the dangers in your weak areas, and do something practical and concrete about them.

The case studies that follow are of two couples who have learned the hard way to plant their own hedges. Their hedges bear little resemblance to mine. That's the point.

Names and insignificant details have been changed to protect identities.

Ryan and Madison Vanderay

Ryan is a successful independent insurance agent in the South. Madison worked early in their marriage but became pregnant almost immediately, and they now have five children under age eleven. They were a passionate, exciting couple during their long courtship, but financial setbacks, health problems, and two miscarriages made early married life difficult.

Seven pregnancies in a dozen years have not been a problem for Madison. She loves babies, was heartbroken over the two losses, and is interested in maybe even having one more. Both Vanderays are active in their local church, serving in Sunday school and in the choir and on various boards and committees. Ryan is also visible in community affairs for the sake of his business.

Ryan has found that Saturdays can be big in his line of work. People who can't see him during the workweek will often schedule a Saturday appointment. Madison pleaded with him to take one day off other than Sunday. So, when his business became healthy enough, he announced he was taking Mondays off.

To Madison, this was heaven. She looked forward to their getting a babysitter and spending the day together, or having Ryan watch the kids while she spent the day shopping and running errands. She had felt so isolated and trapped that she couldn't wait to get away for a few hours.

Unfortunately, the first time Ryan took a Monday off, they had a breakdown in communication. He agreed to watch the kids for a while, and she assumed he knew she would be gone most of the day. But many of his clients had not gotten word of his day off, so he tried to answer calls and do business over the phone while keeping track of the kids. The longer Madison was gone, the angrier Ryan became.

When she got home, he gave her an earful. Not only was she not going to have a free babysitter on his next day off, but he was also going golfing all day. His day off, in case she didn't know it, was for *his* sake, not hers, and that was the way things were going to be.

"When do I get a day off?" she asked. That was a valid question, of course, but it was a mistake to ask it just then.

"You get a day off all day every day," he said. He lived to regret that foolish remark.

When tempers cooled, the Vanderays knew they had a problem. Ryan established on his voicemail that he was unavailable on Mondays. He pledged to babysit from breakfast through lunch so Madison could eat out with friends and get her errands and shopping done. She agreed to let him do whatever he wanted in the afternoon, and if she needed a babysitter so she could go with him or remain out on her own, that was okay. Monday evenings also became their date nights.

"That revolutionized our marriage," Ryan says. "I feel like I'm helping her. I get time to have some fun. She's happier because she gets out, sometimes for the whole day and evening. And even though we're each freer to do what we want, we are also seeing more of each other than ever."

Madison says that Ryan seems like the same young, energetic, funny, creative guy she married. "He's less uptight, and we have fun like we used to. We talk like never before. Sometimes we go somewhere before or after dinner, but often we don't. Sometimes we're the last people they have to shoo out of the restaurant, gabbing and planning and telling each other everything all evening. We've even been known to go and park!"

Logan and Jessica Johnson

I was privileged to work with Logan and Jessica Johnson on a lengthy magazine article about their marriage. I met Logan in the early 1990s when he was a college basketball coach.

A crisis arose when Logan was near the top of his profession—a Division I coach admired and sought after, a speaker, a jogger—in short, the desire of many other wives. Only Jessica knew the truth. He was invisible at home, wrapped up in his work, his speaking engagements, and his physical fitness. He treated Jessica as "the little woman" who was to handle the home and provide the ideal environment for him so he could remain at the top of his game.

A depth of spirituality and character precluded Jessica from looking for another man; it even eliminated from her mind the possibility of divorcing Logan when their troubles began. She admits, however, that she was terribly vulnerable during the crisis and can't say with certainty that she could have fought off the urge to look to someone else if certain circumstances had been in place.

Logan thought he had a good marriage. His wife was beautiful and talented and a good mother. She was a creative decorator, a good cook, a singer—in short, everything a man like Logan could want in a wife.

For years Jessica tried to get Logan's attention. Her methods became more and more drastic as his solutions to her tantrums became more and more predictable. If she complained about his lack of attention or demanded to know why he ignored her in public, if she moaned about his curtness to her or his condescension, or if she wanted to know why he never touched her except in bed or didn't have time to talk to her for even ten minutes a day, he would quickly take the temperature of the situation. If it looked serious, he would apologize, make promises, bring her flowers, take her out to dinner, and see how long that kept her happy.

After six years she had had it, and he didn't even suspect it. She dropped the bomb on him one Sunday afternoon in December. He had killed her emotionally, she said. She told him she would not divorce him, would not leave him, but that neither could she guarantee any emotional response to him whatsoever. He had killed every last vestige of love she'd ever felt for him. She was finished, defeated, deflated, and she couldn't even smile.

It was as if someone had kicked him in the stomach. When he began promising to turn over a new leaf, she simply went upstairs to bed. He knew this was serious and that no bandage was going to make things right again. He wept, sensing, finally knowing, that she was right. He begged for forgiveness from God and for a solution.

Logan was an obsessive, compulsive person, driven to succeed at whatever he set his mind to, whether it meant working out for hours, building a winning basketball team, or speaking a hundred times a year. He could do anything. And now he decided to put his mind to his marriage. He was ready and willing to do whatever it took not just to salvage it but to make it the best it could be. He wept and wept as God brought to his mind dozens of things he should have done over the years. He was reminded of every complaint Jessica had registered, and he filled page after page of a yellow legal pad, determined to change his ways on every point.

God also led him to a book, *Love Life for Every Married Couple*, by Ed Wheat,[1] and he memorized the principles from the author that urged him to apply the *BEST* acronym. He was to bless, edify, share with, and touch his wife constantly, not just to win her back but also simply because it was the right thing to do. In fact, Dr. Wheat stipulated in his book that all this activity would not guarantee any response from the hurting spouse. He said in essence that the wounded partner might never respond after all the damage that had been done but that these principles applied anyway and should be followed.

Logan was desperate to convince Jessica that this was no typical restart. He meant it this time. He had really heard her. He loved her with all his heart and wanted to prove it. He was so committed to his marriage that everything else in his life paled in comparison, and yet she could not bring herself to respond. She couldn't smile or even speak except in cordial, formal, functional conversation. He got no encouragement from her and said he "felt as if I were looking into the eyes of a dead woman, a woman I had killed."

The story continues, of course, and happily. Eventually Logan proved himself. God forgave him and has given him the strength to maintain his commitment to this day. Jessica finally forgave him and saw life and love return to her being. At the time of their marital crisis, they had two children. They have since had two more.

A miraculous transformation has taken place in that home, all because Logan got the message and planted hedges, albeit almost too late.

He talks to his wife a lot every day.

He spends time with her and with the children. He remembers special days.

They date frequently.

He applies a lot of nonsexual touching.

She has become the center of his life.

It hasn't been a quick fix. He knows he can never let his guard down, never slip into the old patterns. Now that he is head coach of an even bigger college basketball program and the family has moved to another state, the risks and temptations are greater than ever. Yet his resolve is all the stronger. Remember, these were not just leaves he turned over. They were hedges he planted deep in thick, rich soil, and they're growing strong.

Other Hedges

Have you ever taken your wife for granted? Maybe you're a funny guy, charming, a storyteller. But she's heard them all. You don't come alive until you have a new audience. At a party you give people eye contact, really listen, and use your best humor and your most charming qualities.

Try something new and different. Try treating your wife the way you would someone you just met.

Scripture is clear that we are to prefer others as more important than ourselves. The Bible says, "Let nothing be done through selfish ambition or conceit, but in lowliness of mind let each esteem others better than himself. Let each of you look out not only for his own interests, but also for the interests of others" (Philippians 2:3-4).

Imagine the impact on your marriage and family if you practiced that at home. Charm your wife. Amuse her. Tell her your best stories. Give her the details from your office that you might otherwise have saved for when you have the floor in a social situation. Look at her, smile at her, wink at her, make it obvious she's your favorite person in the world, not just in the room. And do this when you're alone, too.

Some couples schedule a breakfast out each week. I know a pastor and two business executives who have regular appointments with their wives booked right into their calendars, and their assistants know that those dates are inviolable. They don't feel obligated to tell callers where their boss will be, but they do say, "I'm sorry. That slot is filled."

To a busy man, a regular appointment with his wife is every bit as much of a hedge as the rest of mine are. Spend time talking with your wife. Find out what her deepest needs are, what she really wants and requires from you. Then plant a hedge around that, around her, around you, and around your marriage. It'll be the best gardening you've ever done.

Notes

CHAPTER 2 | THE TWENTY-FIRST CENTURY

1. "How Common Is Pastoral Indiscretion?" Christianity Today's *Leadership*, Winter 1988.
2. "The Leadership Survey on Pastors and Internet Pornography," Christianity Today's *Leadership*, Winter 2001.
3. Ibid.
4. Morgan Lee, "Here's How 770 Pastors Describe Their Struggle with Porn," *Christianity Today*, January 26, 2016.
5. Ray Carroll, *Fallen Pastor: Finding Restoration in a Broken World* (Davidson, NC: Civitas Press, 2011).
6. Heather Griffiths et al., *Introduction to Sociology 2e* (Houston, TX: OpenStax, 2015), https://openstax.org/books/introduction-sociology-2e /pages/14-introduction-to-marriage-and-family.
7. Shere Hite, *The Hite Report on Male Sexuality* (New York: Alfred A. Knopf, 1981).
8. "Morality Continues to Decay," Barna Research Group, November 3, 2003, https://www.barna.com/research/morality-continues-to-decay.
9. "Gen Z and Morality: What Teens Believe (So Far)," Barna Research Group in partnership with Impact 360 Institute, October 9, 2018, https://www .barna.com/research/gen-z-morality.

CHAPTER 3 | THE PRICE

1. George Barna and Mark Hatch, *Boiling Point: How Coming Cultural Shifts Will Change Your Life* (Ventura, CA: Regal Books, 2001), 49.
2. Joni Eareckson Tada, *A Spectacle of Glory: God's Light Shining through Me Every Day* (Grand Rapids, MI: Zondervan, 2016).

3. Mark Twain, *Following the Equator*, vol. 1, "Pudd'nhead Wilson's New Calendar" (Hartford and New York: American Publishing Co. and Doubleday & McLure Co., 1897).

4. Dainis Graveris, "Porn Statistics [2023]: How Many People REALLY Watch Porn?" *SexualAlpha*, May 31, 2023, https://sexualalpha.com/how -many-people-watch-porn-statistics.

CHAPTER 5 | DISTINCTIVE VIEWS OF INTIMACY

1. Miriam Ehrenberg and Otto Ehrenberg *The Intimate Circle: The Sexual Dynamics of Family Life* (New York: Simon and Schuster, 1988), 47–48.

2. Zachary Wagner, "In Search of Non-Toxic Male Sexuality," *Christianity Today*, June 12, 2023.

3. Rachel Joy Welcher, "What Comes after the Purity Culture Reckoning," *Christianity Today*, October 14, 2021.

CHAPTER 10 | TACTILE DANGER

1. James Dobson, *Life on the Edge: A Young Adult's Guide to a Meaningful Life* (Nashville, TN: W Pub Group, 1997).

2. *The Reader's Digest Treasury of Modern Quotations* (New York: Reader's Digest Press, 1975), 82.

CHAPTER 11 | WATCH YOUR MOUTH

1. James Dobson, "The Lure of Infidelity" (audio broadcast), Focus on the Family, 1978.

2. James Dobson, *Love for a Lifetime: Building a Marriage That Will Go the Distance* (Portland: Multnomah Books, 1987).

3. James L. Johnson, *What Every Woman Should Know about a Man* (Grand Rapids, MI: Zondervan, 1977).

4. Said to the author in a private conversation.

5. Ibid.

CHAPTER 13 | LOOKING BACK

1. W. Bradford Wilcox, "The Evolution of Divorce," *National Affairs*, fall 2009.

2. "Born Again Christians Just as Likely to Divorce as Are Non-Christians," *Barna Update*, September 8, 2004.

3. "New Marriage and Divorce Statistics Released," Barna Research Group, March 31, 2008, https://www.barna.com/research/new-marriage-and -divorce-statistics-released.

4. "Divorce Statistics: Over 115 Studies, Facts and Rates for 2022," Wilkinson & Finkbeiner law firm, accessed September 18, 2023, https://www.wf-lawyers.com/divorce-statistics-and-facts.

CHAPTER 14 | *LOVE* IS SPELLED T-I-M-E

1. Mike Bass, *Cincinnati Post* as printed in the *Chicago Tribune*, March 28, 1989, 5.
2. M. J. Amft, "The Vorce and Other Questions," *Campus Life*, January 1978, 43.
3. Donna Kato, "Children Suffer More from Divorce Than Previously Thought," *San Jose Mercury*, June 3, 1997.
4. Judith S. Wallerstein and Joan B. Kelly, *Surviving the Breakup: How Children and Parents Cope with Divorce* (New York: Basic Books, 1980), 33.
5. Ibid., 48.
6. Ibid., 211.
7. "What Are the Effects of Divorce on Children?" FamilyMeans, accessed November 1, 2023, https://www.familymeans.org/effects-of-divorce-on-children.html.

CHAPTER 15 | LOVE'S TAPESTRY

1. James Dobson, *Love Must Be Tough: New Hope for Marriages in Crisis* (Carol Stream, IL: Tyndale House Publishers, 2007).

CHAPTER 17 | DISCIPLINE, CONSISTENCY, VICTORY, TOTALITY

1. Ed Wheat and Gloria Okes Perkins, *Love Life for Every Married Couple: How to Fall in Love, Stay in Love, Rekindle Your Love* (Grand Rapids, MI: Zondervan, 1980).

Study Guide

by John Perrodin

This guide can be used on your own or, for the greatest positive impact on your marriage, with your wife. If you choose to do the latter, it would be helpful for her to read the book as well.

Introduction

A Necessity Bestowed

No Trespassing should be the sign on every husband's and wife's heart when it comes to the relationship God has given him or her to protect, honor, and cherish.

Psalm 89:40 implies that strongholds are brought to ruin when hedges are trampled. Job 1:10 implies that Job was so richly blessed—before God allowed him to be tested—because God had built "a hedge around him, around his household, and around all that he [had] on every side."

Jesus told a parable about landowners who planted vineyards and protected them with hedges. When those hedges were crushed or removed, ruin came to those vineyards.

People are much more precious than land or holdings. If we can keep from deceiving ourselves about our own resolve and inner strength, we will see the need for healthy hedges that keep love in and infidelity out.

Study Guide for Chapter 1
When First We Practice to Deceive

THE TANGLED WEB
Christopher and Ashley convinced themselves that their love was so perfect that God had to be in it. That's often the basis for an affair. God wants us to be happy, right? Ironic then, isn't it, how often we hear that the supposed perfect couple can't hold things together? They've elevated happiness above fidelity and selfishness over commitment.

TAKE ACTION
Take steps now to keep from losing focus on what first attracted you to your wife. Write to your beloved, setting out what excited, interested, and delighted you about her. Accentuate the positive—no negatives or correctives here. Affirm and encourage your wife. Put your thoughts in a card, and slip it under a pillow or post it someplace she'll be sure to find it.

NURTURING THE HEDGES AROUND YOUR HOME
Maybe on a business trip you hung around with a female colleague, and upon reflection, you realize that you wouldn't have wanted your wife to do the same. Maybe nothing improper was said or done, but investing the emotional energy and time was inappropriate.

For a hedge to grow, flourish, and protect, it needs the proper nutrients at the right time. Gardening requires patience, skill, and creativity. Without understanding specific needs, it's impossible to nurture anyone in a meaningful way.

TALK IT OUT

1. Put yourself in your wife's place. Does she struggle with depression? Temptation? Exhaustion? Anger? Fear?
2. How do you cultivate intimacy outside the bedroom?
3. How can you increase emotional attachments to your wife?
4. Discuss how, through secret signs, knowing looks, and special touches, you can stay close to each other.

PLANTING NEW HEDGES

Christopher and Ashley allowed themselves to admire, like, respect, and enjoy each other without a second thought to the dangers of progressive feelings, emotional attachments, or the lure of infatuation. Consider why this was such a problem.

TALK IT OUT

1. Have you ever denigrated your wife, even in jest, to another? Why? When? How did you feel? Did you discuss with her the things you've said to others about her?
2. What hedge could you plant to protect your marriage?
3. Admit to your wife whether you have ever contemplated giving up and what pushed you to the limit.
4. Has no-fault divorce changed the way people think? Discuss why such thinking is antithetical to a biblical marriage.

COUNTING THE COST OF IGNORING HEDGES

Couples committed for life are oddities today. But lifelong commitment should still be our goal, even if it's a tough one.

Fortunately, we can learn from others, benefiting from their strengths and weaknesses. We don't have to make mistakes if we can glean from the errors of those who have gone before us. To Christians, divorce should always be seen as the last possible option.

But it helps to discuss the subject to better understand what's causing pain in a relationship. Or what has killed someone else's.

Consider the unwilling participants in the marriage feast from
Luke 14:15-24:

> Now when one of those who sat at the table with Him
> heard these things, he said to Him, "Blessed is he who
> shall eat bread in the kingdom of God!"
>
> Then He said to him, "A certain man gave a great
> supper and invited many, and sent his servant at supper
> time to say to those who were invited, 'Come, for all
> things are now ready.' "But they all with one accord
> began to make excuses. The first said to him, 'I have
> bought a piece of ground, and I must go and see it. I
> ask you to have me excused.' And another said, 'I have
> bought five yoke of oxen, and I am going to test them.
> I ask you to have me excused.' Still another said, 'I have
> married a wife, and therefore I cannot come.' "So that
> servant came and reported these things to his master.
> Then the master of the house, being angry, said to his
> servant, 'Go out quickly into the streets and lanes of the
> city, and bring in here the poor and the maimed and the
> lame and the blind.' And the servant said, 'Master, it is
> done as you commanded, and still there is room.'
>
> "Then the master said to the servant, 'Go out into
> the highways and hedges, and compel them to come in,
> that my house may be filled. For I say to you that none
> of those men who were invited shall taste my supper.'"

Like those unwilling dinner invitees, couples often neglect
what God has in store for them. They reject the hope of tomorrow
for today's dalliance. While we know the union between husband
and wife is a holy estate, we treat it as a bother, a hassle, an old
garment easily cast off. Rediscover the gift in your relationship.

TAKE ACTION

If many of your friends and acquaintances have fallen in their marriages—people you never would have suspected—how will you avoid becoming a casualty? Talk and pray with your wife about how you will avoid becoming one more statistic. List five reasons you want to experience a lifelong marriage, and then think of five steps you can take toward such longevity.

Study Guide for Chapter 2
The Twenty-First Century

THE CHANGING CLIMATE

Recognizing danger keeps you on the path to victory. Acknowledge infatuation for what it is. Too many deny it. In the workplace, it's common to meet someone with whom there seems to be an immediate bond. You can be married for years and still develop a crush on someone. You like them, they like you, you hit it off. That's the time to be proactive—remember your hedges—before a problem develops. That's why hedges are so important.

TAKE ACTION

In this century alone, several evangelical leaders have fallen prey to sexual temptation. But so have many lesser-known leaders, perhaps someone in your own church. Work with your wife to come up with a list of ten ways society and morals have changed just during the twenty-first century. Discuss why these changes make it harder than ever to stay faithful. Talk about how the body of Christ deals with such disclosures.

NURTURING THE HEDGES AROUND YOUR HOME

Don't treat a new friend of the opposite sex the way you treat an old, respected friend. Refrain from touching her, being alone with her, flirting with her (even in jest), or saying anything to her you wouldn't say if your wife were there. Conversely, friendships with long-admired associates can quickly turn into something more intimate.

Be careful of relationships with members of the opposite sex. Appropriate hedges help you guard against temptation.

TALK IT OUT

1. Discuss the concept of "instant attraction." Has it ever happened to you?
2. What can you do if you feel that surge or charge when you meet someone new?
3. How would you define your and your wife's traditional roles? . . . creative roles? . . . changing roles?

PLANTING NEW HEDGES

We must plant hedges well in advance of even meeting someone else. It's the painless way to protect your marriage. Hedges nip marriage-threatening relationships before they get started.

Sadly, women in record numbers are cheating on their husbands. Why? They are often ignored by busy husbands. Many women throw themselves into their work and find companionship with lonely, unattached men—unless well-tended hedges are in place.

TALK IT OUT

1. What modern opportunities can be marriage killers?
2. List common interests that allow you and your wife to share not only quality time but also quantity time.
3. What do you think about married couples having separate vacations, separate interests, separate finances, and separate beds?
4. What hedge do you need to plant and nurture to strengthen your relationship?

COUNTING THE COST OF IGNORING HEDGES

A man with a perfect wife is still capable of lust, of a senseless seeking of that which would destroy him and his family. If he doesn't fear his own potential and construct a hedge around himself and his marriage, he's headed for disaster.

Consider the familiar story of King David from 2 Samuel 11–12. Though married, David became enamored with Bathsheba, the wife of Uriah the Hittite, one of his military commanders who was off to war. David ultimately committed adultery with Bathsheba and impregnated her. To cover his actions, David summoned Uriah back from the battlefield, hoping Uriah would sleep with his wife, but Uriah refused. So David sent him back to war and ordered that he be placed in a dangerous position in battle, which led to his death.

The prophet Nathan confronted David, who acknowledged his sin and repented. But the couple lost the child who had resulted from their union.

This story serves as a powerful lesson about the consequences of adultery and the importance of repentance and seeking forgiveness. Though David was known as "a man after God's own heart" (see Acts 13:22), temptation overwhelmed him. His only hope, like ours, would have been to run. Second Timothy 2:22 says, "Flee also youthful lusts . . ." Beware the not-so-youthful lusts as well.

TAKE ACTION

Only by understanding mutual weaknesses can a husband and wife truly help each other overcome the shame and pain that accompany them. Confess to your wife privately your personal points of temptation. Be blunt about your struggles. Pray together for strength. Talk about what makes it easier (or more difficult) to resist temptation. Realize that this may be a difficult conversation for both you and your wife, so go gently.

Study Guide for Chapter 3
The Price

THE RAVAGES OF IMMORALITY

Like Jerry's abject disappointment in his pastor at the age of twelve, it's not uncommon to discover that someone you admired and respected has fallen to temptation. You don't want to believe it. You might even initially find yourself in one of the stages of grief: denial or anger preceding eventual acceptance. Every such trauma should make you want to avoid such resulting chaos in your own life.

TAKE ACTION

Taken preventative measures. Plant hedges. Review Joni Eareckson Tada's counsel:

> Some people find our Lord's approach to lust
> unnecessarily harsh. Jesus says, "If your right eye
> causes you to stumble, gouge it out and throw it
> away. . . . If your right hand causes you to stumble,
> cut it off and throw it away" (Matthew 5:29-30,
> NIV). He's not being literal here, but we get the
> idea. When it comes to lust, Jesus prescribes a
> severe, even radical operation.
>
> In other words, this is nothing to coddle or play
> with—just as one would not play with a venomous snake.
> If we don't deal severely with lust, then a glance becomes
> a gaze. A thought becomes an action. A casual fantasy
> becomes heartbreak and a nightmare. So, yes, be harsh
> with such inclinations. Walk away. Avert your gaze. Leave
> the movie. Turn off your computer. These actions will
> result in God's blessing—and spare you years of regret.

NURTURING THE HEDGES AROUND YOUR HOME

Be on guard against finding fault with your mate, as this may be the enemy's way of setting you up for failure. You could be, in essence, building a case to justify straying.

TALK IT OUT

1. Discuss the idea that there are always two sides to a broken marriage. Is this *always* the case?
2. Is it possible, even likely, that only one of the partners has violated their sacred wedding vows?
3. What causes a man with a seemingly wonderful wife to be drawn to another woman?
4. Discuss the upside of living in fear—enough to cause you to flee immorality.
5. What makes an offender blame, or worse, give credit to God for a new fling?

PLANTING NEW HEDGES

Which hedges of Jerry's seem to fit your situation as well? What hedges might be unique to you?

TALK IT OUT

1. What makes otherwise-Bible-believing Christians consider divorce as a possibility?
2. What do you think of the modern inclusion in wedding vows of ". . . for as long as we both shall love"?
3. Discuss the rationalization that "God doesn't want me to be unhappy."

COUNTING THE COST OF IGNORING HEDGES

Jerry mentioned a complex litany of events that take place between a couple's heartfelt vows and adultery. He said the antidote is not praying against such events or even resolving to conquer them but rather following the counsel of the apostle Paul to Timothy and fleeing lust.

TAKE ACTION
We are to run. To get out. To get away. Why? Does this admonition to flee somehow serve as an admission on God's part that He didn't equip us with the ability to subdue our natures in this area? God tells us, "You shall not . . ." (Exodus 20:14), and in the New Testament He says that if we so much as look upon a woman to lust after her, we have already committed adultery with her in our hearts (see Matthew 5:28).

In other areas, God grants us victory. We can win over jealousy, a bad temper, greed, and even pride. We can train our consciences to avoid theft, bad-mouthing, and lying. But in the face of this danger? *Flee.*

Study Guide for Chapter 4
Who Is at Fault?

DON'T BLAME GOD
Understanding how God made us is crucial. As a child, Jerry found that he had a powerful interest in the opposite sex. He wrote, "Had I only known this was normal! That I was not alone! That such attraction to women, yes, even to their sexuality, was God's idea! Is that heresy? It's not now, and it wasn't then. Though I can't recall having completely lustful thoughts in junior high, I carried a deep sense of guilt about even wanting to look at girls."

Some things never change. Men are grown-up boys, each with varying abilities to withstand the lure of an attractive female. Some stop and stare. Others know better. Pretending we don't notice is neither healthy nor helpful. (This is true for our wives as well.)

TAKE ACTION
Celebrate your differences. Is the adage that opposites attract true for you? Talk and pray with your wife about the ways you're the same as well as different. Find common ground in interests, likes

and dislikes, and dreams for the future. Categorize your differences so you can better discern and respect your individual preferences.

NURTURING THE HEDGES AROUND YOUR HOME

Sex is a gift from God. He created men and women to be drawn to each other. Jerry wrote, "I know some people may laugh at my notion of looking at women to appreciate God's creativity and would accuse me of inventing a spiritual reason to leer. I maintain that after years of steeling myself to avert my eyes from something made attractive by God, developing an appreciation for it is far healthier."

Jerry expressed there an honest desire to keep his promise of purity to his wife. But he also knows he will sometimes see beauty that begs a second look. Thankfully, that doesn't have to be the same as lust.

TALK IT OUT

1. Discuss the double standard we all know exists. What happens when you notice that others have noticed your wife? How does she respond to someone else's untoward interest in you?
2. How did God make you? What thrills and delights you?
3. How do you communicate your likes and dislikes to your wife?
4. Describe a chauvinist you've known. How do you differ from the stereotypical male? How are you the same?
5. How do you teach your kids about sex? What's your style?

PLANTING NEW HEDGES

"I was always quick to point out to my sons that the rush of feeling they might experience for a beautiful woman should never be mistaken for true love," Jerry wrote. "Such a rush is a mere infatuation, physical and sensual attraction, a path to a dead end. A relationship may begin with physical attraction . . . but to build an entire relationship on that alone leads to disaster."

Jerry makes the point that any relationship based purely on appearance is shallow and ultimately meaningless. Man looks at the outward appearance, but God sees the heart (see 1 Samuel 16:7). If we exalt appearance over substance, we pervert the natural attraction between the sexes that God planned.

TALK IT OUT

1. Why should a long-lasting relationship never be based solely on physical attraction?
2. What do you do to keep the passion in your relationship?
3. Talk about how nonsexual touching of your spouse can improve a marriage.
4. What hedge do you need to plant and nurture to strengthen your relationship?

COUNTING THE COST OF IGNORING HEDGES

Women need to understand how their dress, appearance, and attitude affect the opposite sex. Women and men usually take different routes to excitement and eroticism. As Jerry explained it: "These differences in attraction actually compete with each other. A man is turned on by the mere thought of a beautiful woman—imagining, fantasizing about the possibilities. When he meets a woman, the scenario has already been played out in his mind." The woman, however, needs more time and attention. She can't be rushed. The bottom line is this: Men and women are not from the same planet. We don't even speak the same language.

Consider the story of Abigail, a life-saving wife found in 1 Samuel 25:14-25:

> Now one of the young men told Abigail, Nabal's wife, saying, "Look, David sent messengers from the wilderness to greet our master; and he reviled them. But the men were very good to us, and we were not hurt, nor did we

miss anything as long as we accompanied them, when we were in the fields. They were a wall to us both by night and day, all the time we were with them keeping the sheep. Now therefore, know and consider what you will do, for harm is determined against our master and against all his household. For he is such a scoundrel that one cannot speak to him."

Then Abigail made haste and took two hundred loaves of bread, two skins of wine, five sheep already dressed, five seahs of roasted grain, one hundred clusters of raisins, and two hundred cakes of figs, and loaded them on donkeys. And she said to her servants, "Go on before me; see, I am coming after you." But she did not tell her husband Nabal.

So it was, as she rode on the donkey, that she went down under cover of the hill; and there were David and his men, coming down toward her, and she met them. Now David had said, "Surely in vain I have protected all that this fellow has in the wilderness, so that nothing was missed of all that belongs to him. And he has repaid me evil for good. May God do so, and more also, to the enemies of David, if I leave one male of all who belong to him by morning light."

Now when Abigail saw David, she dismounted quickly from the donkey, fell on her face before David, and bowed down to the ground. So she fell at his feet and said: "On me, my lord, on me let this iniquity be! And please let your maidservant speak in your ears, and hear the words of your maidservant. Please, let not my lord regard this scoundrel Nabal. For as his name is, so is he: Nabal is his name, and folly is with him! But I, your maidservant, did not see the young men of my lord whom you sent."

TAKE ACTION

Make this a no-holds-barred conversation. Discuss whether Abigail fits the mold of the submissive wife. Was she faithful to her husband or merely concerned about her own skin? Describe ways you've come to your wife's rescue. Talk about how you cover for each other. Highlight your wife's strengths, and contrast them with your weaknesses.

Study Guide for Chapter 5

Distinctive Views of Intimacy

WHAT DO YOU TELL YOUR KIDS?

Despite the pervasive messages the world thrusts upon us, just because it seems like everyone in movies, television, and books jumps into bed with each other at the first opportunity, we must instill in our children the biblical admonition that sex before or outside of marriage is wrong, is sin, and has consequences. That's why planting hedges is paramount.

TAKE ACTION

Jerry admits that his notion of looking at women to appreciate God's creativity could be misinterpreted as inventing a spiritual reason to leer. After years of steeling himself to avert his eyes from something made attractive by God, he believes developing an appreciation for it is far healthier—a distinction worth teaching to our sons and daughters. Clearly it would be wrong to gawk and dwell upon some stranger's beauty, especially after having vowed before God and man to put one's spouse ahead of all others.

NURTURING THE HEDGES AROUND YOUR HOME

Think about and discuss how you can shift the emphasis in your own home from evaluating women by their looks or their attire. Jerry posits that it's generally accepted that women are mostly aroused by environment, atmosphere, tenderness, romance, and touch while men can be aroused merely by their own imaginations.

TALK IT OUT

1. Discuss how the differences in attraction between men and woman can actually compete with each other.
2. Jerry says that a man is turned on by the mere thought of a beautiful woman—imagining, fantasizing about the possibilities. Be open with each other about how this makes you feel.
3. Talk about how your wife might appreciate a man's voice or smile or manner while at the same time he could be lightyears ahead. She smiles innocently at his interest, then he says or does something inappropriate. She's insulted, he's offended, and neither understands what went wrong.
4. Discuss the generalities regarding the differences between men and women—that men are to be the leaders, planners, and visionaries while women are to be submissive, supportive, and reactive. Do you agree or disagree? Why?

PLANTING NEW HEDGES

It's time to reevaluate the so-called purity culture that inadvertently dehumanizes women by treating them as sexual objects and views men merely as sexual animals who can't control themselves. If it hypersexualizes women's bodies, it hypersexualizes men's minds. Zachary Wagner (editorial director for the Center for Pastor Theologians) said, "In a bizarre twist on the prosperity gospel, some Christian teachers have argued that following God's design for sex is the path to your best sex life. Wives are charged to be more sexually available to their husbands as the solution to their struggles with pornography. Single men are told that God's 'provision' for their out-of-control sexual desires is marriage, reducing a covenant relationship to a permissible sexual outlet. Since sexual satisfaction subtly becomes normalized as the rightful inheritance of godly men, certain forms of male sexual entitlement are all too common."

He concluded that "we can aspire to more for men. Not just to stop lashing out in violence or sinking into compulsive sexual behavior, but to become more truly human as advocates for justice, faithful friends, noble protectors, honorable husbands, and selfless lovers. As we look to Christ, the true man, we can become new men."

TALK IT OUT

1. How do you feel about the idea that "men truly couldn't control their lust if women didn't take on the responsibility of dressing and acting in ways that squelched it . . . that the responsibility for sexual sin and temptation—even assault—fell squarely on the shoulders of women"?

2. Is it possible that men and women alike bought into the purity culture that advised women to be submissive to men who were simply wired this way?

COUNTING THE COST OF IGNORING HEDGES

Jerry admits that at times, especially as teenagers, men might wish they hadn't been equipped with an engine that idles like a rocket but isn't supposed to be launched for years. But to hide behind nature to justify aggression and chauvinism is cowardly. Theologians and psychologists can work out the reasons we're made this way. Our task is to channel our drives into something positive and to glorify God in the process.

TAKE ACTION

Don't get the idea that Jerry is suggesting his eyes are always roving and that Dianna can't keep his attention. (He says that anyone who has seen her knows otherwise.) It doesn't take a lingering look to appreciate beauty, and there are more than enough reasons not to stare at other women. First, it would threaten your wife and jeopardize your covenant with her. Second, it would be dangerous to your thought life, because your eyes and mind have no right to dwell there. Even if the woman doesn't belong to anyone else, you do!

Study Guide for Chapter 6
What's in a Look?

THE DYNAMICS OF FLIRTATION

Though flirting seems harmless, it can be both wrong and dangerous. "If someone says something flirtatious to me," Jerry wrote, "my first impulse is to expand on it, play with it, and see how quick and funny I can be. But I resist that. It isn't fair. It's mental and emotional unfaithfulness. I would be exercising a portion of my brain and soul reserved for my exclusive lover." Our time and energy should go toward keeping our own relationship vibrant rather than allowing it to be diffused and diverted by flirting with someone else.

TAKE ACTION

How does your wife respond if you bring her flowers? How does it affect you if she sends you a love note? Talk about how such gestures make you both feel. Explore ways you can love without ulterior motives—including the expectation of sex. List unexpected things you could do to show your wife you're still in love. *Hints:* Take the kids somewhere so she can take a nap; make her breakfast in bed; have a gift delivered.

Suggested assignment: Perform three such random acts of love this week.

NURTURING THE HEDGES AROUND YOUR HOME

If you want to flirt, flirt with your wife. She may not look, feel, or sound the way she did when you first flirted with her years ago. She may not know what to think at first. But your wife still wants to flirt. Try it. Wink at her across the room. Blow her a kiss no one else sees. Play footsie under the table. Give her a squeeze, a pinch, a tickle no one else notices. You'll be glad you did.

TALK IT OUT

1. How do you define *flirting*?
2. How did you flirt with your wife before you married her?
3. How did you flirt on your honeymoon?
4. How do you flirt with her now?
5. Has your flirting become less frequent and less important to you? If so, discuss why.

PLANTING NEW HEDGES

Married couples do not commonly flirt with each other, so this may have to be relearned. Marital flirting is really no different from adolescent flirting. You can do the same things, only everything you're thinking about and hoping will come of it is legal, normal, acceptable, and beautiful. Marital flirting is fun and safe. You can tease your wife about something you'd like to do later—and follow through. What could be more enjoyable?

TALK IT OUT

1. Discuss the difference between a crush or infatuation and love.
2. Describe a time when you've been concerned that someone had a crush on you or your wife.
3. How did you handle that uncomfortable feeling?
4. Now talk about the way you feel when you think of your wife after all this time.
5. What hedge do you need to plant and nurture to strengthen your relationship?

COUNTING THE COST OF IGNORING HEDGES

Flirting starts out fun, funny, and innocent. "I know two men who have left their wives for other men's wives," Jerry wrote, "and it all began with what each party thought was harmless flirting." There's no such thing unless you're flirting with your wife.

As with any other innocent activity that eventually gets out of hand, flirting can be a good and natural part of a person's progression toward true love. God made us able to respond emotionally and physically to attention from the opposite sex, and that's the initial aim of flirting. But like any of His gifts, this is one that can be cheapened and counterfeited, used for evil as well as for good.

Consider this advice from Proverbs 5:15-20:

> Drink water from your own cistern,
> And running water from your own well.
> Should your fountains be dispersed abroad,
> Streams of water in the streets?
> Let them be only your own,
> And not for strangers with you.
> Let your fountain be blessed,
> And rejoice with the wife of your youth.
> As a loving deer and a graceful doe,
> Let her breasts satisfy you at all times;
> And always be enraptured with her love.
> For why should you, my son, be enraptured by
> an immoral woman,
> And be embraced in the arms of a seductress?

TAKE ACTION

Temptation comes in every shape and size. Often we don't even see it coming. Unburden yourself. Discuss the temptations in your life—at work, at home, on the road. Share heart to heart the concerns you have about family, friends, or coworkers who push the line of propriety. If you have acted inappropriately, talk to your wife about the situation and how you can avoid it in the future. You long ago made a sacred vow to remain pure for your wife. Write that promise as you remember it.

Study Guide for Chapter 7
Is This Scriptural?

THE BIBLICAL BASIS FOR HEDGES

Adulterers are liars, and they are as good at it as alcoholics. Jerry told an anecdote about an acquaintance who told him he was seeing a woman other than his wife but that they were just friends. He was not, he claimed, interested in her romantically. They had a lot in common, talked easily, and liked each other's company. Jerry told him he didn't have the right to have a woman as a close friend when he was married and that his behavior was slowly killing his wife. The man seemed convinced and convicted of his sin.

TAKE ACTION

It's tragic to watch the death of a marriage. List some of the high-profile figures you've heard of whose love lives have been grist for supermarket tabloids. What is it about relationships in a fishbowl that are so difficult? Consider how you and your wife are watched by children, family, coworkers, and friends. Discuss ways you can set an example of purity and faithfulness that will have a lasting impact on others.

NURTURING THE HEDGES AROUND YOUR HOME

Jerry said his friend "seemed to see the light" and even promised he would break off the relationship. But that very night, he met the other woman after work. They embraced, kissing, "before they left the state in her car." Jerry continued, "By the time he really came to his senses and pleaded for his wife to take him back . . . the divorce was final. Adultery causes chaos." That's inevitable.

TALK IT OUT

1. What did Jerry mean when he said, "The escape comes with the temptation. It's preventative medicine, not first aid after you've already set your course on a path toward injury"?

2. How do children respond to divorce? Are they resilient, as some so-called experts claim?
3. What are your personal limits of forgiveness? Could you ever forgive your wife for being unfaithful? Why or why not?

PLANTING NEW HEDGES

As much as the addictive streaming services of this century try to convince us otherwise, adultery is not funny. And even though it has become common, it's certainly not normal from God's point of view. The media have convinced many that adultery is hardly more serious than exceeding the speed limit.

"Everybody does it."

"This is a new age."

"Don't be so old-fashioned."

"Get with the program."

Those are the messages we hear too often.

TALK IT OUT

1. It's often said that married couples have better and more frequent sex than live-ins. Why would or should this be true?
2. Discuss the new world of adultery of the mind. Today's temptations come in the form of movies, books, online publications, shows, comics, music, and more online options than we can list. Talk about ways you can overcome the desire to mentally stray.
3. Why does God forbid adultery? What does that say about the marital relationship?
4. What hedge do you need to plant and nurture to strengthen your relationship?

COUNTING THE COST OF IGNORING HEDGES

Why is it so important that couples avoid adultery? Why does Jerry insist that we must build hedges around our hearts, eyes, hands, spouses, and marriages? If the Bible puts adultery in the same class as murder, it is a threat not only to our marriages but also to our very lives.

Consider the admonition to walk in love as found in Ephesians 5:1-7:

> Therefore be imitators of God as dear children. And walk in love, as Christ also has loved us and given Himself for us, an offering and a sacrifice to God for a sweet-smelling aroma.
>
> But fornication and all uncleanness or covetousness, let it not even be named among you, as is fitting for saints; neither filthiness, nor foolish talking, nor coarse jesting, which are not fitting, but rather giving of thanks For this you know, that no fornicator, unclean person, nor covetous man, who is an idolater, has any inheritance in the kingdom of Christ and God. Let no one deceive you with empty words, for because of these things the wrath of God comes upon the sons of disobedience. Therefore do not be partakers with them.

TAKE ACTION

How would you define *filthiness*, *foolish talking*, and *coarse jesting*? How are loose words connected with flirting and, ultimately, adultery? If purity is the goal of every believer, what are you doing to move closer to holiness? Create your own list of ways you and your wife can draw closer to God.

Study Guide for Chapter 8

The Man in the Mirror

THE POWER OF SELF-DECEPTION

The key is preventative maintenance. Once that first step has been taken down the road of self-deceit and rationalization, there's no turning back. Each excuse sounds more plausible, and before he knows it, the typical male has satisfied every curiosity, every urge. Regardless of the remorse, the self-loathing, and the pledges for the future, the pattern will repeat itself as long as he refuses to flee. There is no other defense, no other option.

TAKE ACTION

It's prayer time . . . finally. Amazingly, couples often think they're too busy to pray. But unless you both are connected to God, you can't help but sputter and falter as you seek to build your home on Him. Discuss your top three reasons it's tough to pray together as a couple. Discuss ways to get past these, and then end your discussion with prayer.

NURTURING THE HEDGES AROUND YOUR HOME

No one likes to admit weakness. We'd all like to know someone so spiritual, so wise, so disciplined that he could ignore or throw away a porn magazine left in a hotel room by the previous guest. But Jerry admits that if he didn't throw it out upon first discovering it, ignoring it would be difficult. We don't all share the same trigger points, but we need to acknowledge our problem areas.

TALK IT OUT

1. Discuss why couples carefully construct façades rather than looking at each other eye to eye.
2. Can we really hide who we are from ourselves, others, God? Why do we keep trying to do just that?
3. What's your prayer history? Have you received powerful answers to prayer that should encourage you to continue?
4. List Christian prayer warriors you admire, and explain why.

PLANTING NEW HEDGES

"I do plant hedges against being alone or working too closely with women I simply admire or like," Jerry wrote. "That, to me, is more dangerous. I could see myself becoming attached to or enamored with someone I worked with if I didn't emphasize keeping everything on a professional basis."

TALK IT OUT

1. Is there anything wrong with admiring someone of the opposite sex? Are platonic friendships among adults of the opposite sex possible outside the phony world of entertainment and social media?

2. List your personal hedges to keep business relationships on a professional level. Does your place of employment have standards on this issue? If not, what should they be?

3. Do you find yourself jealous of your wife's relationships? Talk about what would make you feel more (or less) comfortable about them.

4. What hedge do you need to plant and nurture to strengthen your relationship?

COUNTING THE COST OF IGNORING HEDGES

The only future in self-deceit is ruin. Let's quit kidding ourselves. We sometimes have filthy thoughts. No, we don't have to broadcast to the public every base notion and urge, but in our heart of hearts, let's avoid denial. Who are we to think we are above carnal drives and desires?

Consider John 3:19-21:

> "And this is the condemnation, that the light has come into the world, and men loved darkness rather than light, because their deeds were evil. For everyone practicing evil hates the light and does not come to the light, lest his deeds should be exposed. But he who does the truth comes to the light, that his deeds may be clearly seen, that they have been done in God."

Now think about how this relates to Romans 7:14-16:

> For we know that the law is spiritual, but I am carnal,
> sold under sin. For what I am doing, I do not understand.
> For what I will to do, that I do not practice; but what I
> hate, that I do. If, then, I do what I will not to do, I agree
> with the law that it is good.

TAKE ACTION
You can't be helped until you admit you need help. Take time to discuss with your wife your weakness regarding sexual temptations. Be honest and open. List problem areas. Explain your concerns, and get her help, accountability, and prayer support. If necessary, consider meeting together with your pastor or a Christian counselor.

Study Guide for Chapter 9
That Controversial Rule

TWO'S COMPANY; THREE'S SECURITY
Jerry's philosophy is that if you take care of how things *look*, you take care of how they *are*. Logic says that if we're following the biblical injunction to abstain from even the "appearance of evil" (1 Thessalonians 5:22, KJV), we will also abstain from the evil itself. Meetings with the opposite sex should only take place in public or with at least one other person present. That provides protection for everyone involved, first for their reputations and second against temptation.

TAKE ACTION
The idea of abstaining from even the appearance of evil has fallen into disfavor even in certain Christian circles since the turn of this century. Many prefer to dwell on their freedoms rather than hemming themselves in. Work with your wife to develop a practical

policy on how each of you should interact with unrelated members of the opposite sex. Consider what limits would make you both comfortable and keep you from violating each other's sensibilities.

NURTURING THE HEDGES AROUND YOUR HOME

Once, Jerry found out at the last minute that his business travel plans included flying on the same plane and staying in the same hotel as a female employee, just the two of them. Had he known earlier, he would have made other plans. "With a phone call from the airport," Jerry wrote, "I passed the buck to my wife. . . . The fact that I had called her and had made a practice of keeping her informed of such seeming improprieties for years gave Dianna the confidence to immediately agree to the trip." It takes discipline, but we can set patterns of faithfulness that protect our marriages.

TALK IT OUT

1. Tell your wife about times someone has made you feel uncomfortable or crossed an invisible line of intimacy.
2. Talk about why you would or would not keep such information to yourself.
3. If you ever think your wife doesn't recognize the signs of interest by the opposite sex, be ready to talk this out.

PLANTING NEW HEDGES

Jerry includes dining with unrelated members of the opposite sex as a prohibition. Why? Because there's something personal and even intimate about eating with someone. It's a time to relax, to sit close, to open up. If that weren't true, why are so many dates centered on food?

TALK IT OUT

1. Talk about the most romantic meal you've ever shared as husband and wife. What made it special?
2. What is there about intimate conversation over dinner that opens your heart and soul to your companion? Discuss

how such a setting might lower inhibitions and allow for inappropriate topics between coworkers or even strangers.

3. Suggest ways to keep your family close even when traveling. How can a man make his unavailability clear to someone he meets on a business trip?

4. What hedge do you need to plant and nurture to strengthen your relationship?

COUNTING THE COST OF IGNORING HEDGES

Dining and traveling hedges should never be trampled. It's easy to morph into someone we're not when away from home. The price of suspicion is high, and the price of infidelity is even higher.

Consider Ephesians 5:8-14. Note how it urges believers to walk in the light and to make sure that all they do is appropriate and above board:

> For you were once darkness, but now you are light in the Lord. Walk as children of light (for the fruit of the Spirit is in all goodness, righteousness, and truth), finding out what is acceptable to the Lord. And have no fellowship with the unfruitful works of darkness, but rather expose them. For it is shameful even to speak of those things which are done by them in secret. But all things that are exposed are made manifest by the light, for whatever makes manifest is light. Therefore He says:
>
> > "Awake, you who sleep,
> > Arise from the dead,
> > And Christ will give you light."

TAKE ACTION

Plan an intimate dinner for two. Work on the details together, find childcare, and create a completely romantic mini-getaway where you and your wife can relax and talk. Make it a priority to discuss what you mean to each other. Leave problems out of the picture. Make this a time of sanctuary for just the two of you.

Study Guide for Chapter 10
Tactile Danger

TOUCHY, TOUCHY!
"If I embrace only dear friends or relatives and only in the presence of others," Jerry wrote, "I am not tempted to make the embrace longer or more impassioned than is appropriate. I like hugging women. It can be friendly. But if I allowed myself to embrace just anyone, even dear friends, in private, I would be less confident of my motives." Human beings need companionship. That's why the power of touch can be so overwhelming.

TAKE ACTION
List socially appropriate, non-tactile ways to show friendship or affection. Put more simply: How can you show you care about someone of the opposite sex without resorting to hugs or actions that could send mixed messages? Also note which of these you use with your wife, and then consider whether you should find more loving ways of communicating as husband and wife.

NURTURING THE HEDGES AROUND YOUR HOME
Touching and being touched, embracing and being embraced, is as much a matter of common sense and decency as it is of ethnic background and custom. Because of the way Jerry was raised, he treads carefully in this area. If that doesn't happen to be an issue with you, Jerry recommends only that you be sensitive to the attitudes and interpretations of those you choose to touch. Others may have weaknesses you can't sense.

TALK IT OUT

1. Talk about your life as a child. Were your parents affectionate with each other and open with hugs, kisses, and caresses?
2. With regard to physical affection, what kind of home have you both created for your children?
3. What are the good and bad aspects of being physically affectionate with people outside your family?

PLANTING NEW HEDGES

It's not always appropriate to embrace even a Christian of the opposite sex. For some, such openness to touching and hugging can be a problem. Jerry knows people who fell in love because they enjoyed and looked forward to what began as a spiritual expression of brotherly and sisterly love. Done in front of your wife, that might be wholly acceptable, but don't open yourself to such a possibility in private.

TALK IT OUT

1. When you get together with your church family, do you openly show affection? Does such behavior ever cross the line of appropriateness?
2. Do some have difficulty separating the positive feeling of a hug from the sexual connotation that sometimes accompanies it? Discuss how we, as Christians, should be especially careful that we don't make a weaker brother or sister fall.
3. Talk about how you feel about the new openness to physical affection we often see in church. Has this been a positive change? Why or why not?
4. What hedge do you need to plant and nurture to strengthen your relationship?

COUNTING THE COST OF IGNORING HEDGES

Jerry wrote about a friend who spent time in the arms of a friend's wife. What began as seemingly innocent consolation over serious personal problems became a passionate embrace. "My friend was not without fault," Jerry wrote, "but he was weak and vulnerable. Once she had taken advantage of him, there was no turning back. A marriage ended, and an affair began. There was no future in it for either of them, but they still played it out." And it all began with a hug.

Consider Ephesians 5:15-21, where we see that God's expectation for us is that we'll walk in wisdom, not foolishness:

> See then that you walk circumspectly, not as fools but as wise, redeeming the time, because the days are evil.
>
> Therefore do not be unwise, but understand what the will of the Lord is. And do not be drunk with wine, in which is dissipation; but be filled with the Spirit, speaking to one another in psalms and hymns and spiritual songs, singing and making melody in your heart to the Lord, giving thanks always for all things to God the Father in the name of our Lord Jesus Christ, submitting to one another in the fear of God.

TAKE ACTION

Learn from a good example. Think of a couple who have a dynamic marriage, and then identify what keeps their relationship fresh. Note what they do together and what they avoid. Commit to growing your own marital bond and making that connection even stronger. You and your wife should tell each other what positive changes you'd like to make.

Study Guide for Chapter 11
Watch Your Mouth

SOME COMPLIMENTS DON'T PAY

Husband and wife should meet each other's needs, and others should mind their own business. Protect the hedge of marital intimacy.

TAKE ACTION

It's time for a love note. Write your wife a letter describing what attracts you to her. List inside a beautiful card what thrills you about your beloved, and slip it under a pillow or some other place where she is sure to find it.

NURTURING THE HEDGES AROUND YOUR HOME

Jerry bases part of this hedge on his own reactions to how men talk to his wife. Dianna is beautiful. "It makes me proud to see men do a double take when they see her," he wrote. "If they keep staring, though, I stare right back until they notice that she's with me."

The surest way to ward off inappropriate come-ons and to protect your marriage is by openly acknowledging and proclaiming your love.

TALK IT OUT

1. List things others appreciate about your wife.
2. Tell how you make it clear to others that your wife is taken.
3. Discuss ways you could affirm your wife for her wit, attractiveness, and spiritual depth. Talk about how you would feel if you learned someone else was giving similar compliments.

PLANTING NEW HEDGES

"For some reason," Jerry wrote, "it doesn't bother me if a man comments on my wife's hair or makeup or clothes. But if he should say that she looks pretty or is gorgeous or beautiful, that's too personal. Interestingly, either kind of compliment makes her uncomfortable, but she agrees that the personal approach is worse." Be careful that compliments don't cross the line.

TALK IT OUT

1. Discuss compliments that border on being too personal. Talk about why general comments may be within bounds while personal affirmations can be inappropriate.

2. Why do some people seem at ease with compliments and others squirm?
3. What hedge do you need to plant and nurture to strengthen your relationship?

COUNTING THE COST OF IGNORING HEDGES

Jerry wrote that if we run off with another man's wife—even if we do find more pleasure, more romance, more sex, and more of our ego needs fulfilled—there's still the real world to deal with. In fact, the new relationship may be more burdensome than the one we left because of the spousal maintenance and childcare expenses from the previous marriage. If nothing else, divorce can be financially crushing.

Consider the encouraging words in 1 Thessalonians 5:14-18:

Now we exhort you, brethren, warn those who are unruly, comfort the fainthearted, uphold the weak, be patient with all. See that no one renders evil for evil to anyone, but always pursue what is good both for yourselves and for all.

Rejoice always, pray without ceasing, in everything give thanks; for this is the will of God in Christ Jesus for you.

If this is how we're to treat brothers and sisters in the body of Christ, how much more should we encourage and exhort our wives to live for—and live like—Jesus Christ? Note the emphasis on rejoicing. Honest encouragement is one of the best ways a husband or wife can lead the other to "pursue what is good."

TAKE ACTION

A difficult question: Are you more adept at criticism or compliments? Talk this over with your wife. Explore why you're better at one than the other. Commit to improving how you offer praise and give advice.

Study Guide for Chapter 12
Be Careful What You Ask For

LOOKING DOWN THE BARREL OF A LOADED GUN
We've seen it repeatedly. A man hides his true desires behind a cloak of humor. A little crisis, a little honesty, and suddenly years of innocent flirting blossom into an affair. It began supposedly harmlessly.

TAKE ACTION
Here's a chance to do some research. Make a date with your wife to go to the mall, a park, or some other high-traffic area. Hold hands, and look for high-quality examples of flirting. Distinguish between couples showing flirtatious affection and strangers trying to connect. Note differences in approach and attitude. Jot down your findings, and determine what works and what doesn't.

NURTURING THE HEDGES AROUND YOUR HOME
Flattery, flirtation, suggestive jesting, and what we say to our own wives are all shades of the same color. Words can thrill, delight, entice, and excite. Beware the power of the tongue.

TALK IT OUT
1. Why is it so difficult to retract something you've said? Offer examples of things you wish you'd never said.
2. When do you find yourself the most flirtatious? What prompts this, and how can it be discouraged?
3. Is there a line of appropriate commentary that should not be crossed, even with your wife?

PLANTING NEW HEDGES
"We give the lie to the charge that married couples who never fight are probably as miserable and phony as those who fight all the time," Jerry wrote. "We love each other. We don't always agree, and

we get on each other's nerves occasionally, but neither of us likes tension in the air. We compete to see who can apologize first and get things talked out. We follow the biblical injunction to never let the sun go down on our wrath (see Ephesians 4:26)." Dealing with difficulties today prevents greater pain tomorrow.

TALK IT OUT

1. Do you follow the scriptural admonition to not let the sun go down on your anger? Discuss this policy and why it's advised.
2. Define a "healthy discussion" and how you know when you've crossed the line to a heated argument.
3. What do your children learn from you and your wife about how to handle disagreements?
4. What ways have you found to make your apologies more meaningful? If you owe your wife an apology, take the time now to say what needs to be said.
5. What hedge do you need to plant and nurture to strengthen your relationship?

COUNTING THE COST OF IGNORING HEDGES

The real danger of flirtation comes when you pretend to be teasing but you'd really love to do just what you're suggesting. The recipient of the flirting may not suspect the truth behind the humor, but if she responds in kind, there is opportunity for misunderstanding— or real understanding.

Consider what the book of James says about the power of the tongue in 3:2-12:

For we all stumble in many things. If anyone does not stumble in word, he is a perfect man, able also to bridle the whole body. Indeed, we put bits in horses' mouths that they may obey us, and we turn their whole body. Look also at ships: although they are so large and are driven by fierce winds, they are turned by a very small rudder wherever the pilot desires. Even so the tongue is a little member and boasts great things.

See how great a forest a little fire kindles! And the tongue is a fire, a world of iniquity. The tongue is so set among our members that it defiles the whole body, and sets on fire the course of nature; and it is set on fire by hell. For every kind of beast and bird, of reptile and creature of the sea, is tamed and has been tamed by mankind. But no man can tame the tongue. It is an unruly evil, full of deadly poison. With it we bless our God and Father, and with it we curse men, who have been made in the similitude of God. Out of the same mouth proceed blessing and cursing. My brethren, these things ought not to be so. Does a spring send forth fresh water and bitter from the same opening? Can a fig tree, my brethren, bear olives, or a grapevine bear figs? Thus no spring yields both salt water and fresh.

TAKE ACTION

The tongue is clearly an instrument for good or evil depending on who wields the weapon. Put your recent research to use, and get down to some serious flirting with your wife. Incorporate caring signs of affection into your daily relationship.

Study Guide for Chapter 13
Looking Back

MEMORIES

It may be naïve to think that people would remain true to their vows just by repeating them frequently, but who knows? Jerry and Dianna have found this to be a healthy habit. It allows them to better understand and reflect upon what they promised before God, friends, and each other.

TAKE ACTION

Find your wedding vows or a reasonable facsimile, and recite them to your wife. Look into her eyes, and add your own thoughts about why you feel especially blessed by your marriage.

NURTURING THE HEDGES AROUND YOUR HOME

Somehow, some way, we need to ensure that we remain true to our wives. That means working on our weaknesses, shoring up our strengths, and pouring our lives into each other. It's an effort, but it's also a privilege.

TALK IT OUT

1. Discuss how you lay down your life for your wife and family. What could or should you do to make your love and affection even more obvious?
2. Why is it so difficult today for some to remain true to their spouses? Tell each other your secrets for keeping the bond strong.
3. What is your wife's greatest strength? Tell her what you most admire.
4. Explain in your own words why it's a good idea to repeat your vows to your spouse.

PLANTING NEW HEDGES

"I've never understood the long-standing double standard that seems to wink at males' infidelity while holding women in contempt for the same offense," Jerry wrote. "Of course, the breaking of a sacred vow should not be tolerated for either sex." Vows are meant to be honored, becoming more solid and treasured over time.

TALK IT OUT

1. Discuss the double standard Jerry mentioned. Why does there seem to be a growing tolerance for infidelity?

2. What would you do if a friend confessed unfaithfulness to you? What kind of advice would you give?
3. With all the opportunities for temptation online, talk about why the concept of an "affair" is broader now than it has ever been.
4. What would you do if you caught your wife perusing pornography online?
5. What hedge do you need to plant and nurture to strengthen your relationship?

COUNTING THE COST OF IGNORING HEDGES

Adultery is devastating. Marriages that suffer this ultimate loss of trust can never really be the same. We can only imagine what a spouse who has taken back a wife or husband who has slept with another must go through to enjoy the marriage bed again.

As Ecclesiastes 2:10 says: "Whatever my eyes desired I did not keep from them. I did not withhold my heart from any pleasure."

TAKE ACTION

Write a letter together that you will one day give to your children, expressing why it's so important to value your wedding vows. Include both the text from your ceremony and comments that show why you're glad you've remained faithful through the years. This can become a special document you can present to your children on their wedding days.

Study Guide for Chapter 14
Love *Is Spelled T-I-M-E*

QUALITY TIME VS. QUANTITY TIME

Children see a difference in a healthy marriage. Jerry's kids know that he and Dianna are still affectionate and in love and demonstrative about it, even after all the years they've been married.

TAKE ACTION

Consider the broken and blended homes you're familiar with (maybe even your own), and talk about the "might have beens" if the original husband-and-wife bond had never been broken.

Express to each other your commitment to keeping your marriage strong. Pray together for protection of your relationship.

NURTURING THE HEDGES AROUND YOUR HOME

Strive to provide a model of love, caring, and interdependence for your children. Show them what it means to make and keep a commitment, to set out on a lifetime of love with no wavering, no excuses, and no me-first philosophies. Your actions will speak volumes.

TALK IT OUT

1. Define *true love*. Discuss how your definition differs from what our culture calls love.
2. Talk about which commitments mean the most to you and why.
3. List how children benefit from seeing their parents love and care for each other.
4. Do you think a loving couple should ever discuss divorce? Why or why not?

PLANTING NEW HEDGES

"Hedges can do wonders for a family," Jerry wrote, "and this policy of spending mega-blocks of time with the kids each day turned into rich benefits for Dianna and me too. Our time together was more relaxed, less hurried, less pressured, less obligatory." Children grow up quickly. Unless we savor our time with them, one day we'll wake up regretting our selfishness.

TALK IT OUT

1. Explain the difference between quality and quantity time. Which is most important and why?

2. List your favorite things to do alone and with your wife and family.
3. Discuss investing the time to put your family first. What would have to be sacrificed?
4. What things stress you out the quickest? What relaxes you fastest? Talk these over with your wife.
5. What hedge do you need to plant and nurture to strengthen your relationship?

COUNTING THE COST OF IGNORING HEDGES

Make a decision. Set a course. Carve out the time it takes to devote yourself to your wife and children. And plant a hedge that will protect you, her, and them from the devastation of a broken home. Healthy hedges need time to grow.

Consider the famous passage from Ecclesiastes 3:1-8:

To everything there is a season,
A time for every purpose under heaven:

A time to be born,
And a time to die;
A time to plant,
And a time to pluck what is planted;
A time to kill,
And a time to heal;
A time to break down,
And a time to build up;
A time to weep,
And a time to laugh;
A time to mourn,
And a time to dance;
A time to cast away stones,
And a time to gather stones;
A time to embrace,

And a time to refrain from embracing;
A time to gain,
And a time to lose;
A time to keep,
And a time to throw away;
A time to tear,
And a time to sew;
A time to keep silence,
And a time to speak;
A time to love,
And a time to hate;
A time of war,
And a time of peace.

TAKE ACTION

Write your own version of Ecclesiastes 3:1-8. Express what the present time of life means for you and your family. Whether it represents diapers and potty training or driving lessons and college applications, come up with a poignant, perhaps humorous analysis of "The State of Our Family."

Study Guide for Chapter 15

Love's Tapestry

EVERYBODY LOVES A LOVE STORY

It's never too late to recall the details of your early love, but the longer you go without doing it, the easier they are to forget. By telling your stories over and over through the years, you solidify in your mind the things that attracted you to your spouse in the first place. That's a powerful, positive way to nurture romance.

TAKE ACTION

Call your parents, grandparents, or a close friend and their spouse, and ask them to tell you the story of how they met. Reflect on the joy in the storyteller's voice. Talk about what you've heard. How is it similar to your own tale, and how is it different?

NURTURING THE HEDGES AROUND YOUR HOME

"We were married in downstate Illinois and left the next day to drive across the country for a job in Washington state," Jerry wrote. "We spent our first honeymoon night at the Holiday Inn in Peoria. It didn't seem at all funny then, but that gets the biggest smile today when we recount our story."

TALK IT OUT

1. What is the funniest moment you remember as a couple? What makes you laugh?
2. Write out some of your craziest moments as a couple. Discuss how to pass your love story on to your children.
3. What was your honeymoon like? What went very wrong, and what went very right?
4. Recall major events—a child's birth, a baby's first steps, a child's first day at school.

PLANTING NEW HEDGES

"I also vowed to make Dianna laugh," Jerry wrote, "which I've tried to accomplish daily for more than five decades. (If I've failed by the end of the day, I sometimes resort to swinging from the chandelier.)" Humor can keep a couple sane even during tough times.

TALK IT OUT

1. List ways you've brought a smile to your wife's face.
2. Discuss openly with your wife what brings each of you pleasure in the bedroom.
3. Talk over whether the new openness about sexual matters is a good or bad thing for Christian couples.
4. What hedge do you need to plant and nurture to strengthen your relationship?

COUNTING THE COST OF IGNORING HEDGES

Make your love story so familiar that it becomes part of the fabric of your being. It should become a legend shared through the generations. Grow a family tree that defies all odds and boasts marriage after marriage of stability, strength, and longevity. You can succeed with properly planted hedges.

Think about the sweet love story from Song of Solomon 2:10-14:

> My beloved spoke, and said to me:
> "Rise up, my love, my fair one,
> And come away.
> For lo, the winter is past,
> The rain is over and gone.
> The flowers appear on the earth;
> The time of singing has come,
> And the voice of the turtledove
> Is heard in our land.
> The fig tree puts forth her green figs,
> And the vines with the tender grapes
> Give a good smell.
> Rise up, my love, my fair one,
> And come away!
>
> "O my dove, in the clefts of the rock,
> In the secret places of the cliff,
> Let me see your face,
> Let me hear your voice;
> For your voice is sweet,
> And your face is lovely."

TAKE ACTION

When was the last time you made overtly romantic overtures to your wife? Rent a favorite movie, and watch it together in the dark.

Find time to listen to soft music. Choose to add a dose of romance to your life together. Add fresh sweetener to your love story daily.

Study Guide for Chapter 16
Your Legacy

FAMILY BENEFITS

Jerry says he misses the *Daddy* years when his boys were little. Being called *Dad* reminds him of his own father when he was that age. "I tried to play the same role with my boys that [my dad] played with his. . . . He was everything to us." Jerry's father was an example that he's never forgotten and has tried to emulate.

TAKE ACTION

Has your family turned out differently from what you imagined? List the ways that being a father figure has proved more challenging than you thought it would be. Whether or not you have children of your own, think about how important it is to nurture those who find refuge under your roof. What are you doing to encourage them to grow in the Word? Consider how the differing roles of father and mother both contrast and complement each other. Talk over with your wife practical ways to create hedges specific to those vital but varied roles.

NURTURING THE HEDGES AROUND YOUR HOME

It's a truism that time passes quickly. When we were kids, it seemed to take years for something exciting to happen. Now the pages fly off the calendar. Knowing this, you can strengthen hedges by showing love in small and big ways. You can open doors for your wife, tell your kids you love them, read a book to a grandchild while he still fits in your lap. View every day as an opportunity to share kernels of truth with both your wife and the next generation of believers.

TALK IT OUT

1. Discuss with your wife how quickly time passes—and how you can make the most of each fleeting moment.
2. Talk about legacy, and look for ways to share your faith in Jesus Christ with those whose hands will one day rock the cradle.
3. Encourage one another in your strengths, and pray fervently.

PLANTING NEW HEDGES

Try to make your wife smile when she needs it most. Jokes sometimes work, but a soft touch or gentle kiss is another surefire approach. Above all, often tell her, "I love you." Show your wife that she holds a special place in your heart. Be intentional about growing new hedges that protect the love and laughter you share as a couple.

TALK IT OUT

1. Talk about concerns you see in society in general and in your kids in particular. What most worries you about the state of your children's faith?
2. Recall what your children have inherited from each of you. Focus on the positive and powerful gifts you've both shared with your family through the years.
3. Regularly write short notes to your wife with reminders of love.
4. Take time right now to pray for any in your family who are unsaved and need to find faith and hope in the Savior.
5. What hedge should you maintain to show the importance you place on your legacy of family?

COUNTING THE COST OF IGNORING HEDGES

Kids can turn from their faith in what seems like a moment. Where you once held a child who bowed his head with breathless faith, you may now face a smug doubter. Someone who appears to no longer respect her father or mother. Do not fear or lose hope. Pray for the prodigals, and stay connected to God's Word and promises.

Psalm 78:1-6 is a timely reminder of the importance of legacy and offers practical recommendations for keeping your children on the path of truth and life.

A Contemplation of Asaph.
Give ear, O my people, to my law;
Incline your ears to the words of my mouth.
I will open my mouth in a parable;
I will utter dark sayings of old,
Which we have heard and known,
And our fathers have told us.
We will not hide them from their children,
Telling to the generation to come the praises of the LORD,
And His strength and His wonderful works that He has done.

For He established a testimony in Jacob,
And appointed a law in Israel,
Which He commanded our fathers,
That they should make them known to their children;
That the generation to come might know them,
The children who would be born,
That they may arise and declare them to their children.

TAKE ACTION
Legacy matters. Consider the enormous debt we owe the generations who've gone before us. Write a letter (texts and emails are okay too) thanking your parents and grandparents for setting examples of faithfulness to God and their family. Express gratitude for the hedges that held them together and allowed them to remain true to those they loved. And if your forebears are no longer alive, write a note in their honor that you can share with your children, grandchildren, and their children.

If, however, your parents or grandparents weren't sterling examples of faithfulness, try to identify one or two positive traits or habits for which you can legitimately praise them. Likewise, what lessons have you learned from them that have helped make your life and relationships better?

Study Guide for Chapter 17
Discipline, Consistency, Victory, Totality

THE RECIPE FOR SUCCESS
"It's crucial to understand," Jerry wrote, "that the hedges I've discussed have been my own, tailor-made for an oversexed, gregarious, fun-loving, busy person who might otherwise follow his lusts, say things he shouldn't, flirt, forget the most important person in his life, and not spend as much time with his family as he should."

TAKE ACTION
Work with your wife to list some of the most surprising things you've discovered about yourself through this study. In your own words, explain how the hedges concept could work for you. Note areas where you need to see the greatest improvement in your boundaries. Discuss how your hedges will differ from (or be similar to) your wife's.

NURTURING THE HEDGES AROUND YOUR HOME
Some couples schedule a breakfast out each week. Jerry knows a pastor and two business executives who have regular appointments with their wives booked right into their calendars, and their secretaries know those dates are inviolable.

TALK IT OUT
1. Schedule regular time to get together with your wife. You may need to discuss doing what's necessary to make that happen.

2. Talk about how it makes you feel when a friend or business associate misses an important meeting or phone call. List ways you can keep your wife a top priority.
3. How do you let your wife know she's the most important person in your life?

PLANTING NEW HEDGES

To a busy man, a regular appointment with his wife is every bit as much of a hedge as Jerry's are to him. Trim your hedges to fit your own life and lifestyle. Spend time talking with your wife. Find out what her deepest needs are, what she really wants and requires from you. Then plant a hedge and make it happen.

TALK IT OUT

1. Discuss signs that would indicate you're heading for a crash. How do you manifest stress to your wife and family?
2. Talk over with your wife ways in which you can detect a coming crash and what can and should be done to prevent it.
3. Explain to your wife your deepest needs and heartfelt longings.
4. Determine what each of you can do to help the other find greater fulfillment together.
5. What hedge do you need to plant and nurture to strengthen your relationship?

COUNTING THE COST OF IGNORING HEDGES

Know yourself, understand the dangers in your weak areas, and do something practical and concrete about them.

Consider Ephesians 5:22-33 and its straightforward advice on how a husband and wife should treat each other:

Wives, submit to your own husbands, as to the Lord. For the husband is head of the wife, as also Christ is head of the church; and He is the Savior of the body. Therefore, just as the church is subject to Christ, so let the wives be to their own husbands in everything.

Husbands, love your wives, just as Christ also loved the church and gave Himself for her, that He might sanctify and cleanse her with the washing of water by the word, that He might present her to Himself a glorious church, not having spot or wrinkle or any such thing, bur that she should be holy and without blemish. So husbands ought to love their own wives as their own bodies; he who loves his wife loves himself. For no one ever hated his own flesh, but nourishes and cherishes it, just as the Lord does the church. For we are members of His body, of His flesh and of His bones. "For this reason a man shall leave his father and mother and be joined to his wife, and the two shall become one flesh." This is a great mystery, but I speak concerning Christ and the church. Nevertheless let each one of you in particular so love his own wife as himself, and let the wife see that she respects her husband.

TAKE ACTION

Remind yourself why you want to remain true to your wife. Pull out family albums, and go through them as a couple. Review pictures of your children, your happy home, and the fun times you've shared. Renew your commitment to keeping this joy in your life by remaining fully faithful to one another. Seal your promise with a kiss.

MARRIAGE Assessment
BY FOCUS ON THE FAMILY

Keep Growing Your Marriage.

Find your strengths – and opportunities for growth – with the Focus on the Family Marriage Assessment! You and your spouse will get a detailed report on ways to make your marriage even stronger. You'll also get resources that will help you deepen your bond.

Take the Assessment at
FocusOnTheFamily.com/MarriageAssessment